GERAINT THOMAS
HOW A WELSHMAN WON
THE TOUR DE FRANCE

GERAINT THOMAS

THOMAS

HOW A WELSHMAN WON
THE TOUR DE FRANCE

PHIL STEAD

First impression: 2018

© Copyright Phil Stead and Y Lolfa Cyf., 2018

The contents of this book are subject to copyright, and may
not be reproduced by any means, mechanical or electronic,
without the prior, written consent of the publishers.

The publishers wish to acknowledge the support of
Cyngor Llyfrau Cymru

Cover design: Y Lolfa
Front cover photograph: Press Association
All other photographs: Phil Stead unless otherwise stated

ISBN: 978 1 912631 04 9

Published and printed in Wales
on paper from well-maintained forests by
Y Lolfa Cyf., Talybont, Ceredigion SY24 5HE
website www.ylolfa.com
e-mail ylolfa@ylolfa.com
tel 01970 832 304
fax 832 782

Contents

Prologue

I REMEMBER THE moment I fell in love with cycling and the Tour de France. I was in my grandmother's house when I caught sight of a man on the television. He was skinny, emaciated, with an exhausted, haunted look in his eyes. The trunk of his body was white, glaringly so against the dark brown tan which started above his elbows and ran down to his fingerless-gloved hands. He was wearing a pair of black bib shorts which were hanging loosely from his scrawny shoulders. He was the strangest, most captivating sportsman that I had ever seen. His name was Robert Millar and glorious archive footage showed him winning the polka-dot 'King of the Mountains' jersey at the 1984 Tour de France.

The film I saw was *The High Life*, and it portrayed Millar with unflinching honesty as he was cheated out of the 1985 Vuelta a España by a Spanish conspiracy. I bought his replica Panasonic jersey, which I wore on occasional rides to visit my grandmother in Llantrisant. Millar was a Scotsman in a foreign land, out of place among the suntanned Mediterranean gods who dominated the sport. He flew up hills and won stages with a flamboyant style that I would later hear the French call 'panache'. He took risks and cycled from the heart.

From 1986, I followed the Tour religiously every summer on Channel 4. I loved the whole European thrill of it, from the programme's theme tune (written by the Buzzcocks' Pete Shelley) to the insane crowds on the mountain stages. The presenter and commentator was Phil Liggett, a voice synonymous with the Tour for many years. With no Brits to feature, he would cheerlead riders from 'English-speaking nations'. There weren't many of those either, though in 1986, two Irishmen were at the top of the sport. The first was Stephen Roche, who won the Tour in 1987. In those days, it was all about the Tour de France for me, and I only later became aware of Roche's other achievements, including wins at the Giro d'Italia and the World Championships. The second was Sean Kelly, a gruff hardman from a farming family in Waterford. Kelly was a sprinter who won the green Tour de France points jersey four times. But again, I would only learn later about his incredible wins in the classic one-day races. He became a hero to me and now commentates on Eurosport's cycling coverage. Our paths would cross on the 2018 Tour.

As much as I admired sprinters like Kelly and the Uzbek rider Abdoujaparov, I preferred the climbers like Robert Millar, Luis Herrera and Claudio Chiappucci. It was not unusual in those days for climbers to escape for what seemed like hours in the searing heat on lonely alpine passes. This was the glory that thrilled me – heroic bravery and derring-do as the race met the clouds. And I found all that and more in my next idol, a curious-looking Italian called Marco Pantani.

Miguel Induráin had been boring the life out of cycling for years when Pantani appeared. Induráin's tactic was to win the time trial and defend his lead with monotonous excellence in the mountains. He won five Tours in a row between 1991 and 1995. I sat amongst a group of his supporters on the Alpine slopes of Morzine during the 1994 tour and secretly wished he would lose.

Pantani was Induráin's antithesis. He was the first cyclist I had really loved watching since Robert Millar. He would dance on his pedals and fly past competitors at will as the race climbed high. I had never seen a cyclist like him, and when I bumped into him at the end of a stage in the Alps in 1994, my adulation only grew. He was the first Tour de France cyclist that I had ever met, and from that day 'Elefantino' became my hero. I was desperate for Pantani to win the Tour, and in 1998 I had one of the best sporting experiences of my life when I watched him appear out of the mist at the summit of the Galibier and win the race.

Then along came Lance Armstrong and his robotic US Postal team to squeeze the life out of Marco. I hated Armstrong at the time – he was Pantani's rival, and I was always suspicious of his astounding recovery from cancer. My dislike of Armstrong was more down to his lies and bullying than his drug taking. I've always held mixed views about the complex issue of doping, but the barefaced lying of people like him and another Pantani rival, French climber Richard Virenque, sickened me.

Of course it was later revealed that Marco Pantani was one of the vast majority of riders who were loaded with EPO in those days. For a while I felt cheated; that my spiritual experience at the top of the Galibier had been a falsehood.

It drove me away from cycling, but I cried at the news of his death in 2004 and have always considered him a victim of a sick sporting culture. Pantani would have been great if drugs had never existed. I couldn't say the same about other riders of that period. I was reeling from the revelations of *Operación Puerto*, which in 2006 exposed a sport-wide culture of performance-enhancing drug use. I had completely lost faith with the sport, especially as some of my favourite riders had been implicated. During that period, I didn't feel that I could believe what I was seeing.

The formation in 2009 of Team Sky, with its clean cycling promise, drew me back in. The team included a Welshman in its ranks – a young man called Geraint Thomas who had ridden the Tour for Barloworld in 2007. There was a different feeling in 2009 – not only with the formation of Team Sky, but other teams – like Garmin-Slipstream – who espoused a clean riding philosophy. A returning Lance Armstrong looked beatable and I greatly enjoyed watching him lose his invincibility. I felt there was an even playing field and I watched Bradley Wiggins from the top of the Ventoux that year with a new enthusiasm.

I was a rare creature in those days: a Welsh cycling fan who didn't own lycra. Pro-Cycling fans are common across Europe, but in the UK the sport has only historically interested other cyclists. I loved to watch cycling from an armchair, never fit enough to take part at any level. That changed in 2011 when I suffered a life-threatening illness. Morbidly overweight, I developed a couple of blood clots in my lungs and became incapacitated for a long time. During that period, I vowed that if I recovered, I would take cycling more seriously. And I did. I lost 7 stone and became addicted to the sport as a participant as well as a spectator. Over the next few years, I followed the Tour with my bike and rode many of the iconic climbs.

I bought a motorhome and our family holidays would be spent in the Alps or the Pyrenees, riding and fighting for freebies from the promotional caravan. I was witness to some key Tour de France moments and proudly waved my Welsh flag at Geraint and Luke Rowe. I broadened my horizons, travelling to watch famous one-day races like Paris-Roubaix and the great Italian classic, Il Lombardia.

I never really took to Bradley Wiggins or Chris Froome. To this Welshman, they were blocking Geraint Thomas's chances of glory. If Geraint had been at another team, I was sure that he would have emerged earlier as a race winner. I resented Thomas's sacrifices for others, even though he never did. I couldn't imagine him leading at Team Sky and when he announced his decision to forsake the one-day classics to concentrate on stage races in 2015, I thought he was crazy. There was no way he could ever be more than a Top 5 rider in the Tour, so why give up the chance to become a winner in the classics? It's important to remember here that I'm just a fan. I had no insight, no access, no idea what went on at Sky HQ. I had no idea what Geraint thought he could achieve.

The first indication that I was wrong about his prospects came almost immediately, in the Pyrenean stages of the Tour that year. Thomas was climbing with the best and his performance, especially in the driving rain on Plateau de Beille, promised much. Further improvement would come in

2017 when a lean, almost gaunt Thomas took the Tour of the Alps ahead of established Tour riders like Thibaut Pinot, Mikel Landa, and Domenico Pozzovivo. Thomas's newly streamlined physique dramatically improved his climbing and he looked like a different rider from that cherubic-faced lad who had won Olympic gold on the track. But the Tour de France needs more than ability: it needs consistency over three weeks and importantly, the knack of avoiding accidents. Geraint Thomas had a long history of mishaps, mainly unavoidable freak accidents which earned him the nickname 'crash magnet'.

Thomas's first major crash occurred during training in Australia in 2005, when a piece of metal in the road was flicked up into the wheel of his bike. He fell onto his handlebars and ruptured his spleen, which then had to be removed. The 18 year old spent time in intensive care in Sydney, with his family at his side.

Then in 2009, Thomas broke his nose and his pelvis when he crashed over a railing during the Tirreno-Adriatico race. He was highly placed in the 2011 Tour of Britain before a crash took him out of contention. In 2013 he fractured his pelvis again, this time in the very first stage of the Tour de France. Nonetheless, he bravely continued riding, earning his reputation as one of the tough men of the *peloton* as he astonishingly completed the whole race despite his injury.

In 2015, he was well placed when he crashed spectacularly into a telegraph pole on a descent of the Col de Manse after Warren Barguil collided with him. Despite this latest misfortune, he retained his sense of humour. "I feel alright for now," he would joke afterwards. "I guess my doctor will ask me my name soon. I'll say 'Chris Froome'." Two years later, Thomas was taken down in a freak crash in the Giro d'Italia after Wilco Kelderman hit a police motorbike. He recovered to start the Tour de France, only to crash out yet again after wearing the yellow jersey. Thomas was leading at a crucial point of the 2018 Tirreno-Adriatico race when his chain slipped. With no time to recover, he lost the jersey. "I don't know what the stages are of grief, but I'm still pretty angry," he told *Cycling News*.

While Sky's data showed that Thomas was the strongest rider in the team, and possibly the whole *peloton*, he had always worked in the service of another rider. So when cycling journalist Richard Moore claimed the idea that Thomas could win the Tour was 'fanciful', I'm ashamed to say that I agreed with him. There had been too many crashes for them all to be a coincidence. Thomas was accident-prone and had still not proven himself to be able to sustain a challenge on a three-week race. But I was happy to be wrong about that too.

When the Sky team was announced for the 2018 Tour, it seemed designed to help Chris Froome win his fifth title. Geraint Thomas was described as a 'protected' rider, but he'd been awarded that honour in previous races without it amounting to a great deal. Once Froome was named in the team, Geraint seemed destined, once again, to play second fiddle.

Events on the road changed Thomas's status as the race unfolded, and for once, in a perfect storm, everything went his way. The 14/1 outsider gradually raced himself into contention as the scales of fortune rebalanced after years of bad luck. A combination of experience, maturity and supreme ability allowed Geraint Thomas from Birchgrove in Cardiff to realise the dreams that he had harboured since his first session with Maindy Flyers. Maybe Geraint had dreamed of winning the Tour de France one day, but for me the events of 2018 were unimaginable. Geraint Thomas proved that dreams can come true, and I consider myself privileged to have been there to see his victory with my own disbelieving eyes. I witnessed what I consider to be the greatest achievement in our small country's sporting history. This is the story of 25 years as a cycling fan. This is the story of how a Welshman won Le Tour de France.

STAGE 1

Noirmoutier-en-l'Île to Fontenay-le-Comte

THE 1ST STAGE of the 2018 Tour de France began at Noirmoutier-en-l'Île on an island off the north-west coast, known primarily for growing the most expensive potatoes in the world. When the Tour visited in 1999, the island's causeway, which is usually underwater, saw a number of crashes on the slippery surface. The 2018 route avoided the hazardous Passage du Gois, a paved-over sandbank between the island and the mainland, and the stage was set for a sprint finish with only a small climb towards the end.

The day's favourites were the main sprinters: Marcel Kittel, André Greipel and Mark Cavendish. Quick-Step Floors had a formidable-looking sprint train, but their sprinter, Fernando Gaviria, was riding his first Tour and he may have needed time to adjust. There is always a lot of pressure at the start of the Tour, especially as the first stage winner also claims the yellow jersey as the overall race leader. The first stage this year was what is known as a flat stage. This doesn't mean that it is totally flat, of course, but there are no big climbs to speak of and these are generally days for the main sprinters to compete for the win. Everybody knows how the day will play out, and those teams with fast sprinters will aim to control the race to ensure that their man has a chance to sprint for the win at the end of the day. They know that a large *peloton*, with some riders taking turns to ride at the front, will normally be able to close down a small group of riders at will.

The key thing to understand about cycle racing is that riding behind somebody takes approximately 30% less energy than cycling in front. This can vary depending on speed, wind-strength, etc., but it is a constant factor in the race. I had watched cycling for over a decade, well aware of this law of physics, and thought I understood it well enough, but it wasn't until one day in the mid 1990s that the importance of riding in the slipstream of other riders was hammered home to me.

In my mid twenties, I decided that I wanted to take cycling a bit more seriously and set about joining a club. After a few rides with the Cardiff JIF club, I knew that I was well out of my depth. I asked Ian, the owner of my local bike shop, if he could recommend a more sedate group that I could join. He suggested the Cardiff 100-Milers club, and I met up with them one Sunday morning in a car park at Maindy.

There were about a dozen riders in the car park, mainly old or middle-aged men. They seemed unconcerned by cycling fashion and wore a mismatch of old kit, riding a variety of bikes. One or two of them carried a large satchel on a rack, and some of them actually had bells on their handlebars. Oh no, this wasn't it at all. I would be far too good for this lot. Nonetheless, I deigned to ride out with them.

We left Maindy to travel towards the Bwlch mountain in the Rhondda Valleys. I was shocked when the group rode straight up the busy A470 dual-carriageway out of Cardiff. This was dangerous, surely? I had always stuck to back lanes and minor roads, but here they were confidently crossing Gabalfa roundabout, forcing cars to give way as they rode north.

The group split quickly into pairs and I was told to stay at the back. I did this, pleased with myself as I comfortably spun my pedals as the pace picked up. I wasn't used to riding with somebody alongside and I felt a bit uneasy when cars beeped and shouted out of their windows. The 100-Milers were unconcerned and shouted back or ignored the abuse.

We soon passed Taff's Well and approached Pontypridd. I had been sitting at the back while other riders spun off and took turns at the front of the group. Some of the riders at the front were older than my grandfather, and I was desperate to take my turn. Surely I should be sharing the work – that's what I had seen riders do on the television. I noticed the pace drop a little as we met a headwind. Some of the old boys seemed to be struggling a bit. I decided to ignore orders and take my turn at the head of the group. When a gap came, I pulled around the outside and took my place at the very front.

BANG!

I immediately took the full impact of the wind, and suddenly this was a different game. I was forced to double my efforts and buried my head low into what felt like a gale. I would guess we were travelling at about 16 mph, which is nothing to a serious rider, but to me it suddenly felt like I was sprinting. My heartbeat rose quickly and I was gasping for air. I could hear the other riders chatting amicably about this and that while I felt like I was racing for the finish. I ploughed on – my head near my bars and my back bent double as I moved onto the rivet of my saddle. My legs burned and my arms began aching as I gripped the bars. I blew up. I couldn't take any more, and in utter humiliation I slunk to the back of the group and hung on while I recovered from the effort. I stayed there until we hit the Bwlch and licked my wounds. That was the day I really learned about the effects of wind-resistance, and it transformed my understanding of road racing. I also learned to respect other riders.

On a flat day at the Tour, once the breakaway group has disappeared up the road, the other teams can almost relax. On a day like this, teams with sprinters will share the workload at the front to keep the gap between the break and the *peloton* at a manageable distance. The sprinters themselves, of course, will be sheltered until the last few kilometres of the race, known as 'the final'. Teams with a top sprinter often include what is known as a 'sprint train' in their team. This group of riders forms a protective line in front of their sprinter as the pace picks up towards the finish. The last man to pull over before the sprinter emerges to battle for the line is known as a 'lead-out man'. The legendary sprinter Mario Cipollini was one of the first to utilise a fully-fledged train to win 12 sprint stages of the Tour de France in the 1990s. Until then, sprinters had been less organised, often relying on a single lead-out man to support their sprinter.

Mark Renshaw is a lead-out man. He is probably the best cyclist in that role in recent years, especially known for his work for Mark Cavendish. In this interview with *Cycling Tips*, he explains the anatomy of a sprint train.

> We use two or three guys rotating on the front, trying to keep the speed very high at the 20 km mark. They'll ride down to 10 km to go and then we'll try to bring in a couple more guys. Then 10 km out it's Cav, myself and whoever's in front of me. It depends on what's happened. But there's at least three guys saving themselves with 10 kms to go.
>
> So basically until 10 kms to go, you got everyone working except for three guys. They try and keep the speed high, stay to one side, stay out of the wind, and neutralise the race if there's any attacks. 3 kms to go is usually a pretty decisive time. That's when all our guys are doing their last turns. Tony [Martin]'s always been the guy that gets us to about 1.5 km–1 km and then the guys have to try and get me as close to the front as possible. I usually try to go no more than 1 km out... If you take for example last year, 650 m to go was the point where I'd start my lead-out. You want to keep the speed as high as you can so you don't get swarmed by other riders. I'm on the side of the road, out of the wind. That's the other big thing. The big goal is to bring Cav up to 200 m or 250 m.

The pressure of the first stage often creates danger for the main overall competitors, riders fighting for position on the road and taking big risks as their pent-up energy is released in the excitement of the day. This year was no different. Dramatically, there was a crash with 10 km remaining which saw some of the main contenders delayed, with Chris Froome ending up in a ditch a few kilometres later. Quintana punctured, but for once Geraint Thomas stayed out of trouble and, finishing safely with the main group, found himself almost a minute ahead of his teammate after just one stage.

Colombian Fernando Gaviria took the win and the yellow jersey to announce himself as a new sprinting force in the Tour, but it was the chaos behind him, and the resulting time gaps to Richie Porte, Adam Yates, Nairo Quintana and crucially Chris Froome, on the very first stage, which would prove significant to the outcome of the 2018 Tour de France.

"The first 180 km was fine. It was just the last 20 which was a bit bonkers," Geraint Thomas said. "We missed the main crash and then Egan and Froomey had a bit of bad luck. I was in the front, luckily, out of trouble." Thomas then added a comment which showed where his priorities lay: "It wasn't the end of the world. He was with Richie and Quintana was behind him, so arguably his two strongest rivals." At this early point in the Tour, Thomas wasn't even thinking about his own race. He was there to work for Froome.

Mouilleron-Saint-Germain to La Roche-sur-Yon

I USUALLY PLAN our family summer holidays to coincide with the Tour route. However, this year, things were a little bit arse-backwards. Stage 2 would finish in La Roche-sur-Yon in the western coast Vendée area, which we often visit for the seaside part of our holiday. But I was still in Wales at the start of July. I did manage to visit the area after the end of the Tour and noticed visible signs of the race's presence three weeks earlier. A yellow bicycle was still chained to a lamp-post. A local *boulangerie* was still offering a range of yellow, green and polka-dot cakes. A school was still flying its Tour de France bunting and signs directed visitors to now-empty car parks. These post-tour scenes were recreated across France as people clung onto the memories of their big day.

As soon as the race route is leaked, usually a few days before the official announcement, host towns and villages make plans for displays and events to mark the visit. The whole town will make an effort to be *en fête* for a few weeks around July. This makes it a pleasure to catch the Tour as it passes through any place on the route. Ironically, the most impressive efforts I've ever seen were in Yorkshire for the 2014 Tour, where villages were consumed by the visit. I stood at bars selling specially produced 'King of the Mountains' beer in polka-dot painted pubs next to ingenious hay-bale grandstands erected in roadside fields. The second stage in 2018 offered a day in the spotlight for unremarkable French villages like Saint-Pierre-du-Chemin, Pouzauges and Les Herbiers. They wanted to look their best when the Tour came to town and crowds lined the streets. It had been 80 years since a stage of *La Grande Boucle* last finished in La Roche-sur-Yon.

The stage was won by Peter Sagan, one of my favourite riders. Sagan is a genuine superstar, especially in his home country of Slovakia, where he is revered. On this day, he was wearing the rainbow-striped World Champion's jersey, which is my favourite piece of kit in any sport. The white jersey features the rainbow stripes of green, yellow, black, red and blue; the same colours that appear in the rings on the Olympic flag and which represent the *Union Cycliste Internationale* (UCI). The jersey is worn for a year by the rider who is world champion in their particular discipline. Sagan had won the UCI Road World Championships for the third time in 2017 and Tom Dumoulin would later wear his World Champion skinsuit for the Time-Trial stage, as he was the current World Champion in that speciality.

One of the things that I enjoy about Sagan is his outrageously dated European adverts for Bora kitchens, his team sponsor. In some of these promotions, Sagan cooks dishes on sparkling chrome hobs – my favourite Sagan recipe is sea bass. This year, his team have a co-sponsor, Hansgrohe, who make taps and showers. This has led to even funnier clips as the whole team of Bora-Hansgrohe riders take turns to tell you in awkward detail why they enjoy having a shower.

I'm a little embarrassed to admit that cycling sponsorship works on me. When we renovated our house a few years ago, I sought out flooring from Quick-Step. I wash my hair in Alpecin shampoo and I used to get my insurance from Chris Boardman's team sponsor, Gan, in the early 1990s. I am sure that if I am ever in need of a second-hand luxury watch, then Watchfinder.com would be my first destination as a reward for their ubiquitous advertising during the 2018 Tour – though I do agree with my Tour companion, Scott, that they missed a trick by not naming the company Watchfinder General.

Sagan took the yellow jersey from Gaviria, winning a reduced sprint after a big crash had taken out many of the day's favourites with 2 km remaining. There are no time differences gained by delays caused by any crash in the last 3 km of the race and those affected are given the same time as the winner. But Sagan had gained a 10-second bonus for the win and it was enough to put him ahead of the Colombian. A second crash for Adam Yates in the first two days of the Tour, along with two of his Mitchelton-Scott teammates, meant that Froome, Porte, Quintana and Yates were already around a minute down on Thomas. But for now, Team Sky's focus was still on regaining time for Chris Froome after he had lost 51 seconds in the first stage, as shown in these comments from the team's *Directeur Sportif*, Nicolas Portal.

It's something a bit new. Well, we had that situation a bit in the Giro for a while, but in the Tour it's something different for us. Chris is 51 seconds down. OK, we need to gain time, that's for sure. It's going to be in the Team Time Trial, we hope, and... in the mountains, or maybe even in the crosswinds. We have to take some time back. When you look at Chris's Tour de France victories, except maybe last year, he's often had a big advantage, and you're trying to ride a little bit safer because it would be stupid to race hard, hard, hard. So it's something a bit new.

Stages are often enlivened with one or more intermediate finish lines set up at points where riders can earn bonus seconds or points towards the green jersey competition. If you find yourself near the route of a flat day's stage, it can be worth making for one of the intermediate sprint points, listed in the detailed route plan published on the Tour website. Though these are rarely hugely exciting, it does give some focus and a little interest to a day which otherwise might see the riders pass you by as if on a casual Sunday club ride.

A rider like Thomas would not normally concern himself with any effort to take points or time at one of these intermediate sprints, but today was different and I raised an eyebrow when he competed for a second's bonus. It seemed to belie his comments about serving Chris Froome. Maybe Froome's time loss had already raised doubts about leadership?

"We were up there and no one was going for it," explained Thomas. "Gilbert went and no one else seemed to follow, and I was like, 'I'll go, then.' I was there, so I went. It didn't take any effort, and I'm not going to turn down a second." It was not a hugely significant incident, but it did serve as an early indication of his ambition in this Tour.

Team Time Trial – Cholet to Cholet

I'LL BE HONEST: I hardly ever watch Team Time Trials. I've got little interest in cycle technology or the physics of aerodynamics and I don't know enough about cycling technique to appreciate the minute details of rider position or pedalling style. Add to this a pointy helmet and half-face visor which often completely masks the rider's identity and you can maybe understand why this discipline leaves me cold. Admittedly there is something attractively futuristic about the cycles and the kit, but there is a clinical approach to time trialling which has more to do with physics and science than it does to the romance of sport. And I am a fully-fledged romantic.

But from a purely sporting perspective, the Team Time Trial (TTT) of Stage 3 of the 2018 Tour de France was one of the most keenly anticipated days of the Tour. Away from the mountains, it was this day, more than any other, where significant time gaps would be guaranteed. Due to the individual time-trialling strength of Team Sky's riders, it was possible – even probable – that Geraint Thomas would take the yellow jersey at this very early stage of the race. Thomas was placed in 6th overall and only 15 seconds down on Sagan. The stage was 35 km long, which could allow Team Sky to gain significant time on weaker teams. After all, the TTT at the Critérium du Dauphiné had kick-started Geraint Thomas's overall victory in that race a few weeks earlier.

The inclusion of a TTT in a stage race affects rider selection as a team will need to include strong time-trialling experts to gain time or limit losses for each team member in the overall General Classification (GC) competition. But there was a new rule which meant that team selection was even more important than usual. Addressing concerns that dominant teams (in other words, Team Sky) had made cycling too predictable, there was a change in 2018. In order to liven up races and ostensibly to increase rider safety by reducing the size of the *peloton*, each team would now be reduced from nine to eight riders. But with the biggest budget in world cycling, Team Sky included the strongest selection of time triallists in the Tour. They focussed especially on the Team Time Trial, which could greatly influence the outcome of the whole race. An exceptional array of talent was selected to support Froome.

Jonathan Castroviejo is a 31-year-old Basque rider chosen for his ability to contribute in the Team Time Trial. The Spanish TT champion had been signed from Movistar on a three-year contract in 2017. He was also a powerful *rouleur* and a good climber, making him an excellent choice for the Tour.

Michał Kwiatkowski is a former UCI Road World Champion who was also a member of Omega Pharma–Quick-Step's World Champion Team Time Trial team in 2013. In 2017 he won the Milan-San Remo classic and Strade Bianche. Kwiatkowski is known as one of the classiest riders on the tour and has been heralded by some as a future Tour winner.

Gianni Moscon is a young Italian who signed back in 2015 on the recommendation of Fausto Pinarello, whose company makes the team's bicycles. A winner of the Arctic Race of Norway, Moscon's short career has been dogged with controversy. In 2017 Team Sky admitted that he had racially abused FDJ rider Kévin Reza, and suspended him for six weeks. He was also accused of purposely crashing into a rider in a different race, though that investigation was dropped due to lack of evidence. Moscon is the current Italian Time Trial Champion, and another who would shine in the TTT stage.

Two other riders were not selected for their time-trialling ability but would give their all before pulling over to save their legs for another day. Like Moscon, **Wout Poels** also joined Sky in 2015, winning the team's first classic one-day race with his victory in Liège-Bastogne-Liège in 2016. The Dutchman is one of those riders that might excel in another team as competition for Froome. As it is, he has earned a formidable reputation as a super-*domestique*, excelling in the mountains.

Luke Rowe needs no introduction to the Welsh reader. A childhood friend of Geraint Thomas, Rowe is one of the strongest characters on the Tour and is Team Sky's road captain, a role that often goes to the most experienced riders.

He would prove invaluable on this Tour, taking huge turns at the front of the *peloton* to control the race for Sky.

Next was 21-year-old **Egan Bernal**, the latest in a long line of exciting Colombian climbers to grace the world stage. Dave Brailsford has admitted that he signed Bernal as one for the future. "I've searched and searched for the rider that might be the next Chris Froome, who would be our next big leader for Grand Tours. My choice was Bernal, whom we absolutely had to have in the team. He's our future." The young debutant was to prove invaluable in Sky's attempts to win the 2018 tour.

And then came **Geraint Thomas**, the rider who would step into the breach should Froome crash, or show any weakness after the Giro. Thomas was there as probably the best support rider in the world, and Sky's 'Plan B' – or, as some insisted, their 'Plan G'. Thomas's selection was inevitable. His strength in the Team Time Trial, as the reigning British Time Trial Champion, was clear.

"We'll try to get the stage win first, and if I do end up in yellow, then that would be a really nice bonus," admitted Thomas ahead of the stage, "But the main thing is to go full-gas for the stage win."

The day's action would take place around the city of Cholet in the Loire Valley, a place famous for its red-and-white handkerchiefs. Written in 1897, Théodore Botrel's song 'Le Mouchoir Rouge de Cholet' (The Red Handkerchief of Cholet) became the unofficial anthem of the area. For the arrival of the 2018 tour, Cholet produced a range of specially woven yellow handkerchiefs.

For this team time trial, every rider who finishes in the front group takes the same time as their fourth-placed finisher. Riding in close formation, they work together, with each rider taking a turn at the front of the rotating line. There is no benefit to a single rider finishing well ahead of his teammates. Stronger time triallists will often measure their efforts to ensure they do not drop the weaker riders, while taking longer turns at the front of the group. Even if a rider is unable to take a turn at the front, it can benefit a team if they sit at the back of the group. Wind-tunnel tests show that a rider who sits closely behind aids the aerodynamic progress of the rider in front.

BMC Racing won the stage with an incredible average speed of almost 55 kph. At some points in the race they touched 80 kph, which is pretty scary when you consider that the team are riding bikes which are not designed for handling or safety. The aerodynamic handlebars of a time-trial bike protrude straight forward and a rider's nose will be inches behind his teammate's saddle the whole way round.

Team Sky were booed and jeered as they left the ramp, and setting an aggressive early pace, they soon dropped first Rowe and then Poels. The remaining six riders finished together to take the lead on the day, but it was not enough to win the stage. BMC finished just 4 seconds ahead of Team Sky, but it was enough to put their rider Greg Van Avermaet in the yellow jersey, just 3 seconds ahead of Thomas on the overall classification. Peter Sagan was unable to keep up with the stronger time triallists in his team and finished two minutes behind, conceding yellow. Team Sky did not win the stage, but damage was inflicted on some of their rivals. Vincenzo Nibali, Romain Bardet and Primož Roglič all lost a minute due to the poor performance of their teams in this specialist discipline. Tom Dumoulin's Sunweb team finished just 7 seconds behind Sky.

Geraint Thomas was philosophical when asked about his failure to take the yellow jersey:

> To be honest, I didn't even think about it. It was all about trying to win the stage, and that would have been a nice bonus on top of it. We really wanted to try and get that stage today because we've been close in the past in Tour TTTs. Close, but not quite quick enough. It's a bit frustrating because I felt like I could have had a bit more in the tank by the end.

With so many Time Trial specialists, why did Sky lose out to BMC Racing? Well, there was a suggestion that Chris Froome was suffering a little after his crash on the first day, but BMC had also targeted this stage and had prepared specifically with the Team Time Trial in mind. They designed new shoes, new skinsuits, and had recced the course a week earlier and again on the morning of the race. The team wasn't filled with national champions like Sky but on a technical course, and starting later from the ramp, they were able to judge their effort perfectly.

STAGE 4

La Baule to Sarzeau

STAGE 4 OF the Tour was earmarked as another sprinter stage. The profile was flat and for Team Sky it would be a matter of staying safe and ensuring that Geraint Thomas and Chris Froome lost no time. A stage like this may seem insignificant to viewers of the highlights of the race each evening, but riders on the team will have earned their wages over the day.

Cycling is a team sport. Even though a single rider wins the race, it would be impossible to do so without their team. In other team sports, each member has a chance of glory – in football, even a functional full-back might score a goal from a corner. But in cycling, the *domestique* rarely has their moment in the spotlight, as Luke Rowe explained to BBC Sport:

> You go for three weeks and you know you're not going to get one single opportunity or a snippet of a chance for yourself. It's all for someone else. That's the way cycling is.

There are jobs to do throughout the day – riding in the wind, collecting bottles from the team car, dropping back to help a punctured rider – and the team is selected to include riders who can fulfil specialist roles. There is often speculation about the make-up of the team, with long-term plans affected by injury, form and recent performances.

Team Sky's announcement on 3rd July was clear. "Chris Froome will be supported on the roads of France by Egan Bernal, Jonathan Castroviejo, Michał Kwiatkowski, Gianni Moscon, Wout Poels, Luke Rowe and Geraint Thomas." It was understood from the announcement that Kenyan-born Froome was the rider chosen to aim for yellow in Paris. There had been serious doubts about Froome's participation after a leaked report in December revealed that he had tested with twice the permitted level of the asthma drug salbutamol at the 2017 Vuelta a España. Froome continued to ride while under investigation and won the Giro d'Italia after an astonishing solo ride on the Colle delle Finestre, when the race looked beyond him. Salbutamol is a *specified substance*, which means the World Anti Doping Agency (WADA) agrees it could enter an athlete's body inadvertently. Commonly administered in an inhaler, salbutamol is not banned, nor does it require a Therapeutic Use Exemption (TUE) for normal use. However, it can act as an anabolic agent and increase muscle mass in certain cases.

In a team statement, Froome said:

> My asthma got worse at the Vuelta so I followed the team
> doctor's advice to increase my salbutamol dosage. As always, I
> took the greatest care to ensure that I did not use more than the
> permissible dose.

Sky's lawyers reportedly presented 1,500 pages of expert evidence in his defence. The UCI cleared Froome on July 2nd, just days before the Tour de France, announcing that "the results do not constitute an adverse analytical finding." The race organisers, Amaury Sport Organisation (ASO), had tried to stop him riding, but the UCI's decision now cleared him to compete. Legendary French rider Bernard Hinault had called on riders to strike if Froome was allowed to race the Tour.

The ongoing controversy was significant for Geraint Thomas, because it meant that he had been prepared by Team Sky to take over as leader in the case of Froome's absence. Thomas had spent time at high-altitude training camps in Lanzarote and his training had been focussed on the Tour de France. Froome's attempt at both the Giro d'Italia and the Tour de France in the same year was also considered a little risky. Thomas would be ready if his teammate showed any ill effects from May's race in Italy.

Of course, even though Froome was cleared, there was huge resentment amongst the French public and some cynical commentators. But I have watched cycling in the days of EPO, blood transfusions and human growth hormone. If our biggest doping scandal now involves overuse of an asthma inhaler, then I can live with that.

Greg Van Avermaet began Stage 4 in yellow after BMC Racing's TTT success. There were more crashes, which affected a whole raft of GC (General Classification) riders. Dan Martin, Jakob Fuglsang, Bauke Mollema, Mikel Landa and Steven Kruijswijk were involved in a crash with 50 km to go. Another with 5 km left involved Ilnur Zakarin and Rigoberto Urán. Luke Rowe drove the Sky team at the head of the *peloton* in the final stages to ensure that Geraint Thomas stayed out of trouble while Colombian sprinter Fernando Gaviria took his second stage. Nobody ever celebrates a rider crashing, but in an attritional race like the Tour de France, there were already a lot of Thomas's competitors who were losing time while he stayed upright.

STAGE 5

Lorient to Quimper

I'VE TOURED BRITTANY twice by cycle. The first time was in 1991 after buying my first decent bike, a Raleigh Touriste, from Reg Braddick's shop in Roath. That old shop was a Cardiff landmark, opening in 1945 and running for 70 years until its closure in 2015. I paid £300 for that bike, a fair amount in those days. I remember Reg trying to discuss it with me, but I was completely ignorant. "You do realise you're buying a good bike here, don't you?" he asked. I had no idea about bikes, and I still don't. But I knew Reynolds 531 tubing was considered good, and I loved the Campagnolo groupset. That's all you're going to get from me on cycle parts. I'm already out of my depth.

That first trip was a bit of a disaster. I was travelling with a female colleague in the hope that something more than friendship might develop en route. She bought an identical bike and we went on training rides. Everything was going great until she found herself a new boyfriend days before we left. She still wanted to continue with our holiday plans as we were 'just mates', after all. Her boyfriend wasn't too keen on the idea, and neither was I, to be honest. We argued for two whole weeks and at one point, I'm ashamed to admit that I left her on her own to throw a tantrum while I cycled ahead 15 miles to the next village. Our trip finished in Paris with a crazy dash around the Arc de Triomphe in rush hour to make our train home at the Gare du Nord. Cardiff traffic would never again worry me.

The second trip, in 1995, was more successful. This time I went on a borrowed Jack Taylor tandem with a new girlfriend. It is said that a tandem holiday will either break or make a relationship. Well, it made ours, and we have just celebrated our 20th wedding anniversary. Tandem riding is a taxing discipline requiring patience, teamwork and good humour. As I was struggling to keep the bike upright, Mair would be commenting on the field of sunflowers that we were passing. As I sweated and grappled with the bars on a long climb, she would be waving to passing children. I accused her of not pedalling, and she prodded my arse in protest. Our fortnight around the St Malo area was a huge success and not even a terrifying crash when our back wheel collapsed on a busy dual carriageway affected us too much. We simply hitched a lift in a passing truck and carried the one-wheeled bike home in the guard's van of a train.

We revisited Brittany again in 2018, a short time after the Tour finished. After a few days in Quiberon, I drove our motorhome to Lorient, which had hosted the start of Stage 5. But I was there to visit the Festival Interceltique. The festival had decided with great foresight that this year would be the Year of Wales, and I'd heard good things about the event. While I enjoyed the atmosphere and a performance by Welsh-language band Yr Ods, it appeared that Celticness was viewed a little differently by other countries. In the main parade, thousands of people marched around Lorient in vintage national costumes. To many of those people, Celts were historical, and the festival gave them a snapshot of a forgotten culture. For most nations, Celtic culture belonged to the past.

At night we wandered around the various music venues. Fiddles and clogs were ubiquitous, and excited audiences clapped along to the beat of the bodhrán. Meanwhile in the Welsh tent, we saw an avant-garde jazz band, and a synth-heavy pop group. I left feeling that Wales and Welshness is alive and well, with a strong identity. And yet, still I was surprised to come across many French people who did not recognise our flag. Even watching the Tour, with Geraint Thomas prominent, I was asked several times about the red dragon. And somehow the Basques in the Pyrenees, where rugby is so popular, were also unfamiliar with the flag that I was carrying. And all this just two years after the Euro 2016 tournament, where the Welsh football team reached the semi-finals.

One of the problems with this Welsh identity issue is that Thomas rides with a Union Jack on his sleeve, and television graphics display the letters GBR after his name. I am sure this British identity played a large part in the booing of a rider who has always been popular among riders and fans alike. That is not to belittle the huge part that British Cycling has played in his career development or to insult his British teammates, it's just that Geraint Thomas is Welsh, and he feels Welsh. In the

2008 Olympics, it was announced that neither competitors nor supporters would be allowed to carry the red dragon, or any other flag besides the official ones of the teams competing. As he said at the time:

> It would be great to do a lap of honour draped in the Welsh flag if I win a gold medal, and I'm very disappointed if this rule means that would not be possible.

When Thomas won the 2014 Commonwealth road race for Wales, his pride was evident:

> I was buzzing to compete for Team Wales. I just got stuck in and it couldn't have got any better. Carrying the flag tonight will be a massive honour – that is just as good as winning a race and that means a lot to me and my family.

Luke Rowe admitted the same in an interview with Tom Cary in 2017:

> I love representing GB, I love representing Sky, but representing Wales is potentially just that little bit more special, being a patriotic guy.

The protests that faced Geraint Thomas and Luke Rowe at the start of Stage 5 in Lorient were partially because they wore the British flag of Team Sky. I sensed more hostility on the road this year than I ever had before. I love the French, and I have always found them fair and honourable, shouting their encouragement – *courage!* and *chapeau!* – to riders of all nations. I think Brexit was partly to blame for the new animosity, as well as increased nationalism in France itself. The French are irritated that Sky dominate their national race with what they consider to be stifling, boring tactics, and they are showing their displeasure. Eager to find an excuse on which to pin their frustration, they protested Froome's presence after the salbutamol case, and jeered his team. Before the start in Lorient, Luke Rowe grabbed a protestor's placard which read 'Sky Go Home'. Rowe is not a man to be intimidated and has earned the team captain role by right, often demonstrating his strength of character on the road. The French protests did not have the desired effect, drawing the Team Sky riders closer together and creating a siege mentality. They would look after each other.

The protestor, Didier Bregardes from Lorient, gave some insight into French attitudes when he spoke to *The Guardian*:

> I've nothing against Froome or the riders but it's the way the manager of Sky, Dave Brailsford, dealt with the Froome case. It's insulting what Brailsford said about Lappartient, about him being a small mayor of a small town.

A few days earlier, Team Sky Principal Dave Brailsford had escalated an ongoing spat with the recently elected President of the UCI, Frenchman David Lappartient, who had been the long-serving mayor of Sarzeau (where the fourth stage of the Tour ended), saying of him:

> I gave him the benefit of the doubt when he started. I thought, 'OK, he is new to the job, he obviously doesn't quite understand the responsibilities of a presidential role.' But I think he has still got the local French mayor kind of mentality.

Brailsford might have had a point after a series of ill-advised comments made by the new president about Sky, including suggestions that their wealth had bought expertise to defend

39

Froome's salbutamol case. But it was difficult to know why he would raise the stakes in this way. The French public were angry enough, without Brailsford fanning the flames. Even the outspoken Lance Armstrong could not understand it. "Dave, man," he advised on his podcast, "put the fucking shovel down. Get back in the bus and shut up."

The stage was set for the *puncheurs*. Neither flat enough for the sprinters to be confident, nor mountainous enough for the pure climbers, the rolling terrain would suit all-rounders – those who excelled in the Spring Classic races. Riders like Greg Van Avermaet, Julian Alaphilippe and Peter Sagan would be favourites for the stage.

I watched that uphill stage finish in the kitchen at work, with a colleague who was fascinated by the apparent chaos of the final sprint. "Anybody could win this," she said as a large group came into the final bend. "Nah," I predicted patronisingly. "That bloke in the green jersey will win." She watched with her mouth wide open as Peter Sagan came from six places back to cross the line in first position. I looked at my friend, gave a cocky wink, and sashayed back to the office.

"Everyone knew that was going to be a tricky finish today," said Froome. "But Tom Dumoulin is the guy that stands out at the moment as he's still quite far ahead of me. His team rode a good Team Time Trial and he hasn't lost time." Froome didn't mention his teammate Geraint Thomas, who still lay 52 seconds ahead of him, and just 5 seconds behind Greg Van Avermaet, still in yellow.

STAGE 6

Brest to Mûr-de-Bretagne

STAGE 6 TOOK the riders inland from the western coast of Brittany. As the first step of its passage across northern France, the route passed eastwards from Brest to Mûr-de-Bretagne, where Cadel Evans had won a stage on his way to claiming the 2011 Tour. Although Evans is very much an Australian, I tweeted him as a joke in 2009 to ask whether he had any Welsh heritage. To my surprise, he replied.

> @cadelofficial @pjstead me Welsh? My names – both Cadel and Evans – are Welsh. Evans bloodline? Don't know much of its history. Sorry.

Cadel must have done some more research, because now many sources refer to his Welsh great-grandfather. Some claim the rider was named after various Welsh medieval kings called Cadell, others that Cadell was a Welsh explorer.

Seven years later, the Tour de France arrived at the same town and Geraint Thomas was quietly riding the perfect GC race. He was picking up small amounts of time whenever he could, even on seemingly inconsequential days before the first mountains. Stage 6 was hilly and finished by climbing the steep Mûr twice, but it was not expected to create time gaps in the General Classification. However, both Tom Dumoulin and Romain Bardet suffered late mechanicals which saw them lose time on Thomas. The Dutchman conceded 50 seconds, which would prove decisive later on. He was given a further 20-second penalty when it was ruled that he had drafted behind a team car in his efforts to regain time. Things were not going well for Dumoulin. He had lost a valuable teammate in Michael Matthews, who had withdrawn with illness the day before, and his right-hand man Wilco Kelderman had pulled out due to injury before the start of the Tour. If he was going to challenge Froome and Thomas, he would have to do it with a weakened team.

Thomas also gained another two seconds on Dumoulin at a bonus sprint 12 km from the finish. These seconds would all add up in the final countdown. He looked lively and alert on the final climb, first covering Richie Porte's move then chasing down Dan Martin before looking around for his leader, Froome, saying after the race:

> I managed to sneak a few bonus seconds again. I don't think they'll let me do that for a third time now. But in the final, Dan Martin was super strong. I didn't fancy sprinting for third against Valverde, so I thought I'd save that 1% for another day.

The Irish stage winner Dan Martin is a wonderful, thrilling rider. He races on instinct, attacking with panache, and offers a throwback to the exciting days before cyclists were controlled by instructions from their earpiece and wattage displays on their power meters. Martin is an all-or-nothing rider who launches attacks with reckless abandon. I always find myself cheering him on as his toothy grimace betrays the extent of his efforts. "I like riding in the red," he said, "because I know I can go deeper into the red than the others." I wish he was Welsh, but his cycling pedigree is a mix of Irish and English. His father, Neil Martin, was a double Olympian, and his uncle is Stephen Roche, the famous Irish cyclist.

Chris Froome showed a hint of weakness when he finished slightly behind the group of main contenders who followed Martin home. One rider in the group which gained unexpected seconds on Froome was Vincenzo 'The Shark' Nibali. The Bahrain-Merida rider was one of Team Sky's main challengers, and had already won the Tour in 2014. Nibali also had other Grand Tour scalps – the Giro d'Italia in 2013 and 2016, and La Vuelta back in 2010. I've always admired Nibali – yes, he can climb, but he excels in tough, dirty, hard one-day races. His performance on the wet cobbles in Stage 5 of the 2014 Tour de France was a major factor in his victory that year.

I wanted to see Nibali on his own turf at one of my favourite races. The Tour of Lombardy is historically the last race of the pro season, held in the Como region of northern Italy in early October. Its autumn date has earned it the title 'The race of the falling leaves'. Often held in changeable autumnal weather, it is one of the most beautiful races in the calendar. But there is another reason why the race, now rebranded as 'Il Lombardia' attracts many devotees of the sport from across the world – it is also the site of Madonna del Ghisallo, the patron saint of cyclists and home of the best cycling museum in the world. The race features a steep climb out of Bellagio, a picture-postcard village which sits on the banks of the stunning Lake

Como. This famous climb is named after the church of the Madonna del Ghisallo, which sits at its summit. This climb has historically been the decisive point of the race and has featured in many editions of the Giro d'Italia.

The church's connection with the Giro led La Madonna del Ghisallo to be declared the patron saint of cyclists in 1949, with confirmation from the Pope. The shrine now contains a small cycling museum, bursting with extraordinary photos and artefacts from the sport. Visitors have left hundreds of heart-wrenching messages and tributes to cyclists who have died or been killed on the road. A visit to the chapel is a very moving experience, and an eternal flame burns in the centre of the tiny building. The crumpled bike of Como rider Fabio Casartelli is also on display. I will never forget seeing that terrible crash as I watched the Tour on a small television screen during that tandem holiday in France in 1995. To be reminded again here over 20 years later was very sobering. The old church exudes sadness, especially to those visitors who do not possess the crutch of religion to offer comfort. It can be a difficult place to visit, as I discovered when I went there during the trip to watch the 2015 edition of Il Lombardia, but I'd recommend anybody to make the pilgrimage to this unique, evocative site.

In 2010 the Museo del Ciclismo opened at the same site. It has developed into the world's best cycling museum, with an astounding collection of cycles and memorabilia. I spent over an hour drooling over kit and equipment from dozens of Giro d'Italia winners, including Marco Pantani, Fausto Coppi and Gino Bartali. But we didn't watch the race from the climb of the Madonna del Ghisallo, which featured early that year. We drove instead to stand on the Muro di Sormano, which has become one of the most iconic climbs in Italy.

Starting from the quiet village of Sormano, its slippery, narrow path climbs through the woods for less than 2 km, but it reaches a fearsome 25% gradient towards its summit. It is a beast of a climb, up a greasy path painted with large-print quotes from legendary champions. It was extremely busy on the day we visited and the huge excitement which exploded when the first riders appeared is one of the best experiences I've had as a cycling fan. Rider after rider grappled with their machine as they willed their pedals to keep on turning up that fearsome hill. Nibali attacked on the descent with wild abandon to win the race that day, and become one of my favourite riders. He won Il Lombardia again in 2017, and Milan-San Remo in March 2018. The former Grand Tour winner is now a one-day specialist, but was he still considered a genuine contender for the 2018 Tour de France.

And who were the other contenders? Well, Chris Froome was the big favourite, and it was felt that Richie Porte was likely to be his main challenger. Porte's BMC team was strong and would take time in the TTT. The 33 year old was in good form, having won the Tour de Suisse, and could climb with the best. If he could avoid crashing like he did in 2017, then surely Porte would be up there.

Nairo Quintana was another threat to Froome; but sharing leadership of Movistar with two other riders, Valverde and Landa, could he rely on the 100% support of his team?

Quintana had won the Giro d'Italia and La Vuelta, but the Tour de France had so far eluded the Colombian climber.

Romain Bardet was the local favourite. He had finished on the podium in both 2016 and 2017, and finished third behind Geraint Thomas in the Critérium du Dauphiné. He was a lovely, fluent climber, but he was not the best time triallist.

Primož Roglič could time trial, and climb too, but he lacked experience. Now aged 28, he had entered the Tour for the first time in 2017 and came up with a stage win. The former ski jumper was an outsider for the win, but he could contend for a podium spot.

In my eyes, Tom Dumoulin was the man that could run Froome close. Dumoulin has the consistency, he had won the Giro in 2017 and he was the current World Champion time triallist. He can climb and has an unerring discipline which often sees him apparently dropped, only to re-emerge at the head of a race. Dumoulin is the archetypal modern power-meter rider and would prove difficult to shake off.

STAGE 7

Fougères to Chartres

JULY 13TH, 2018 was the 51st anniversary of the death of English cyclist Tom Simpson. World Champion in 1965 and winner of several one-day classics, Simpson was a rider in the prime of his life when he rode the Tour de France in 1967, aged 29. Sharing a room with his friend, Welshman Colin Lewis, he had been ill on the morning of a very hot day with formidable climbs ahead. The route that day would take the riders across Mont Ventoux, the *Géant de Provence*, one of the most fearsome climbs in France. Lying 6th overall, Simpson was determined not to quit. But suffering from exhaustion, the heat and the brutal climb, the popular rider collapsed near the summit of the Ventoux and was airlifted to hospital, where he died later that day. An autopsy revealed a mixture of amphetamines and alcohol in his body at a time when there were no doping controls on the Tour.

I went to pay tribute to Simpson's shrine late in the 2009 Tour. I wasn't cycling at the time and knew I would need to arrive early if I was going to drive the top of the Ventoux. I flew to Nîmes, hired a small car and made for the climb the evening before the race. There were already traffic jams in the small village of Bédoin, which was bursting at the seams with cycling fans. As I drove up through the woods at the foot of the climb, makeshift bars were serving beer to hundreds of revellers to the beat of blaring Europop. It was more like Glastonbury than a cycling race. After a long drive alongside hundreds of amateur cyclists, the woods receded and I saw the famous bald summit of the Ventoux for the first time. I pulled up on a side road near the famous Chalet Reynard restaurant, about 6 km from the summit, where dozens of television trucks were parked and a giant screen had been erected. Over half a million people would watch the race on the Ventoux that year.

I had a terrible night's sleep in the front seat of that VW Polo on the edge of the mountain. Not only did I dream of falling down the precipice a few feet from my car door, but a stream of drunken Dutch fans walked back and forth until dawn. I hiked up to the summit under the remorseless sun, unforgiving even at that time in the morning. Mont Ventoux is an eerie, barren, inhospitable place, not made for humans, and certainly not made for cycling. By the time I got to Simpson's memorial, I understood better the terrible circumstances of his death. I stood for a while in contemplation and removed my hat. Hundreds of people had left water bottles at the stone as a symbolic offering and dozens of club cycling caps lay in tribute.

51 years to the day after Simpson's death, Stage 7 was the longest of the 2018 Tour, covering 231 km as it continued the eastern path out of Brittany. It was a classic transition stage, designed to move the *peloton* around the country without any

great feature to the day's racing. Although it wasn't pan flat, it would undoubtedly be a stage for the sprinters, with a slightly uphill finish. I confidently predicted another win for Sagan. I felt I was speaking from experience as, after all, I had raced against a top-level Tour de France sprinter in 2014.

That particular year, I didn't have to travel far to enjoy one of my favourite ever trips to see the Tour de France. The first stage of the Tour would finish in Harrogate, Yorkshire, and we drove across the night before the race to camp at the start, in the grounds of Harewood House near Leeds. Yorkshire did the Tour proud and every village was bouncing – flags flew, yellow bicycles hung from lamp posts and white walls were painted with red polka dots. Yorkshire was transformed. The atmosphere was incredible all over the county as locals embraced the event with gusto. We drank warm 'King of the Mountains' ale and feasted on Pantani Pork Pies.

After we waved off the race at Harewood House, I jumped on my bike and rode to see the finish at nearby Harrogate. The Tour in Yorkshire drew a lot of fans who were absolutely new to cycling, with no experience of watching from the road. The event was well policed and stewarded, but spectators were a little confused. They darted back and forth across the course after the main *peloton* had passed, thinking the race was over. But riders followed for several minutes in ones and twos after a chaotic day's racing across the Yorkshire hills.

In the confusion, I kept an eye out for the *Voiture Balai*, the 'broom wagon' signifying the very end of the race convoy. I shouted at stewards that some riders were still out on the course. But five minutes passed, then ten, and I noticed a few amateur cyclists coming by. There were no team vehicles or press and the road seemed very quiet. People were looking around, unsure of the situation – and so were the marshals lining the road. More amateur cyclists passed and I decided that I must have missed the *Voiture Balai* as it was almost 15 minutes since I'd seen a rider. An old lady next to me shrugged her shoulders. Then she wheeled her ancient bike onto the road and cycled slowly towards town. Her steed was an upright sit-up-and-beg shopper with a coiled-sprung leather saddle and a chain guard. She carried her lunchbox in a wicker basket which hung from the front handlebars. I decided to join her, and we set off at a sedate pace towards Harrogate.

I was enjoying the spin along the wide Tour de France route. The crowds were laughing and waving and it was great fun to follow the race home, imagining myself as a rider on my way to victory. Then suddenly I was awoken from my reverie by a deafening siren and the loud growl of a police motorbike, which made me jump out of my skin. I didn't have much time to react before I was overtaken at huge speed by a large man in full kit, cycling at about 35 mph. He shouted a warning, whistled past me and narrowly avoided the teetering old lady and her shopping bike. It was then that I noticed the number pinned on the cyclist's back, and realised that he was the famous Italian sprinter Alessandro Petacchi, a winner of 48 Grand Tour stages. I pulled to the side, mortified at having unwittingly taken part in the Tour de France. I found out later that Petacchi had appealed and the commissaire had reduced his time gap due to crowd interference.

Luckily for Dylan Groenewegen, I was not on the road in

2018 when he won the long Stage 7 to Chartres. No crashes and very little incident meant that the overall leadership remained unchanged. It was a long, even boring day, where no racing took place until the last few kilometres. "You could be forgiven for thinking this was a bike *ride* through northern France, rather than a bike *race*," apologised ITV's Ned Boulting.

Dreux to Amiens

ANOTHER LONG TRANSITION stage would take the riders north towards the Belgian border. By the end of the stage, the *peloton* would have ridden almost 600 km in three days. Nothing, of course, compared to the longest ever stage, which covered 482 km in a single day in 1919, but still a long time in the saddle. Perversely, these long days are seen by the riders as an opportunity to relax until the teams with sprinters wind things up late in the stage. It was also the most French stage of the race, taking place on Bastille Day and finishing in Amiens, home town of the president, Emmanuel Macron. Bastille Day is a huge occasion every year for the French and they crave a local winner. In 2017, Breton Warren Barguil became the first French rider to take the Bastille Day stage in 12 years.

I love being in France on Bastille Day. To be fair, I love being in France on any day. My Francophilia began on a school exchange in the mid 1980s, when I spent a week in Nantes. I developed a crush on pretty, lavender-scented Veronique, ate croissants and drank bowls of hot chocolate for breakfast. I studied French at school and later, during summer holidays, took a job as a claretblazered holiday rep escorting coach tours around Europe. The drivers were French and my language skills improved.

I hear a lot of people complaining that the French are arrogant or rude, but that has rarely been my experience. Maybe it's because I speak the language, but they've always been welcoming to me. In the past 20 years, the vast majority of our family holidays have been spent in France. We've had beach holidays, Eurocamp chalets, caravans and now an old motorhome. France offers everything you could want – beaches, mountains, villages, cities, great food, drink and the best campsites. I'd love to live in France and hopefully that will become possible one day. My favourite region is Brittany, even though it often gives me a terrible foretaste of a future when, like Breton, the Welsh language might just be a memory, remembered mainly in café names and street signs.

Dylan Groenewegen spoiled the French party in 2018 by taking his second consecutive stage win at Amiens. Both Fernando Gaviria and André Greipel were disqualified after two separate incidents in the final sprint. Gaviria, boxed in by Greipel, appeared to headbutt his rival's back in retaliation. Earlier, Greipel seemed to have done some headbutting of his own, involving Nikias Arndt. Incidents like this are pretty common as sprinters fight for their place on the road. Stakes are never higher than at the Tour de France, and tensions sometimes boil over. In 2010, Mark Renshaw tried to headbutt New Zealander Julian Dean, and was thrown off the Tour. Peter Sagan was disqualified last year for an elbow which caused Mark Cavendish to crash out of the tour. My favourite sprint battle took place in 1997 when Belgian sprinter Tom Steels aimed his water bottle at Frenchman Freddie Moncassin. Sprinters tend to be the most aggressive riders, but occasionally fights happen on the climbs. There is a famous clip of two cyclists brawling in the 1995 Vuelta. Leonardo Sierra and Ramón González Arrieta totter about, swinging ineffectual haymakers at each other. One spins a full 360°, catching the other with the back of his hand. I think I would rather take a beating than suffer the indignity of fighting in my cycling shoes.

Another potential podium finisher was affected by a crash on the way to Amiens. Dan Martin came down and lost over a minute. He was not considered a prime challenger to Team Sky, but he had looked very impressive on the Mûr-de-Bretagne, and the injury would do him no favours ahead of the forthcoming stage across the cobbles to Roubaix. As Geraint Thomas said:

> I've got a bit of a sore arse already, so the thought of all those cobbles coming up isn't the most exciting, but you have to grit your teeth and go for it. It's going to be a day to make your bones rattle. The whole day is going to be full-on. Full gas.

STAGE 9

Arras to Roubaix

STAGE 9 WOULD follow part of the route of the legendary Paris-Roubaix one-day race, including 15 sections of cobbles, or *pavé*, as the French call them. The modern Paris-Roubaix race starts in Compiègne, 50 miles north of Paris, and finishes in the famous Roubaix velodrome, close to Lille on the Belgian border. The race travels over old cobbled roads, which have deteriorated badly over the years. At one time, these paths were improved, but cycling fans complained that the new, smooth roads were boring. The course is now maintained by *Les Amis de Paris-Roubaix*, who make sure the cobbled sections are kept in perfect, haphazard, untamed condition.

The race is known as *L'Enfer du Nord* (Hell of the North), earning this sobriquet after the region suffered terrible damage during World War I. I first became aware of it after watching the classic cycling movie *A Sunday In Hell*, and dreamed of one day visiting to experience the atmosphere for myself. And so it was that in 2015 I drove all day from north Wales to the border of France and Belgium, so that I could watch the race with my own eyes.

I had planned my trip down to the last detail. Arriving at the start town of Compiègne, I booked the last room in a dodgy hotel in the worst part of town, near the main train station. Strolling across the bridge to the town centre, where an amateur nocturnal circuit race was taking place, I found a completely different atmosphere. Local riders entertained the crowds, who watched from café tables, drinking the best Belgian beer and eating syrupy bacon waffles. After a good night out in the company of other cycling fans, I walked back to the seedy train station where two men stepped out from the shadows of an alleyway to confront me. The bigger man was about to attack me when they were distracted by a shout from across the road and ran off. I shook off the incident with a quick pastis in the hotel bar before retiring to my smoke-stained room, ready for an early start.

A cycling memorabilia fair had been organised in Compiègne to precede the morning start of the race and I spent over an hour going through the amazing stalls and displays. Europeans seem to collect cycling paraphernalia like we collect football souvenirs. There were old copies of *L'Équipe* reports, race-worn kit, cigarette cards, models and vintage bikes. I just loved it, and spent some considerable time drooling over the woollen 1950s jerseys and evocative photographs from cycling's past.

It was then on to the team presentation in the main square. Thousands had gathered to see the riders sign on and a booming PA warmed up the crowd with interviews and music. Promotions staff fired out rolled up T-shirts from plastic cannons. I caught one and, embarrassingly, celebrated to myself with a fist pump. The presentation itself was an awkward affair, with bored riders lazily lifting a hand in recognition as their names were announced. The strange band of middle-aged Team Sky groupies made their presence known and riders looked at them with distracted amusement. On that stage with their skinny legs and big trainers, they looked like a hundred disillusioned strippers, there to be gawked at. They just wanted to start the race.

I took my place on the barriers, with the start line literally inches from my feet. Riders began to gather and I chatted with a few, who were waiting for their big day to commence. Then the *peloton* rode off slowly behind the race director, who waved a big flag from his convertible, and I rushed to my car to follow the race as it disappeared out of town.

Now started the Wacky Races. I joined a convoy of team and press vehicles which were all careering north towards Roubaix. Within 10 minutes the *peloton* passed over us on a bridge spanning the motorway. I was making for the Trouée d'Arenberg, where the most famous section of cobbles dissects the villages of Wallers and Hasnon. The race was due to reach Arenberg a few hours after I left Compiègne. The long straight, surrounded by the trees of Arenberg Forest, features some of the most irregular cobbled roads in the race. Cycling fans come from all over the world to stand here, and crowds of approximately 10,000 line its 2.4 kilometres – it's a bucket-list destination for any cycling fan. I parked my car in the village of Hasnon and unfolded my Brompton bike, cycling the short distance to the route.

The atmosphere in the forest was electric. The biggest

crowds had gathered at the entrance to the cobbled sector, where a large screen showed the race while fans drank beer and ate giant meaty hot-dogs. This is where the party was happening, and I was more than disappointed to be driving that day. Instead I took my place in the centre of the forest, where there were no barriers and only a piece of rope separated us from the *pavé*. The cobbles on this Napoleonic pathway were even bigger than I'd expected. Large chunks of stone jutted out from all angles in places, with a smooth line difficult or even impossible to follow. I took out the Brompton, to cheers from the crowd, and tried it myself. I juddered along for about 100 metres with fans on either side shouting, *"Allez, allez!"* I was living the dream.

A huge roar signalled the approaching race and motorbikes growled through, followed by the riders. It was as chaotic and exciting as I had imagined. There was no *peloton*: this was every man for himself, and they rode at a breathtaking speed across the jagged blocks of stone. Dusty, sweaty faces grimaced and many bodies showed signs of injury, bloodied limbs and grazed backs giving an indication of earlier crashes. I waved my Welsh flag high above Luke Rowe and Geraint Thomas as they passed.

I rushed off on the Brompton soon after the riders passed, still buzzing from the euphoria of experiencing the race at close quarters. The car journey onwards towards Roubaix was great fun too. To the right, riders charged through dusty roads in front of flag-waving crowds. To my left a few minutes later, a small group navigated their way through fields, and at one point I saw Bradley Wiggins cross a bridge over my head. At various points en route, cars had stopped and lined up at the side of the road to watch the race go by. I drove on to Roubaix, exhilarated.

Roubaix is a working-class industrial town near Lille. It is not a salubrious area and I was advised not to leave my car anywhere vulnerable. There were major diversions in place as I drove around the ring-road towards the centre. After passing through a leafy residential area, the road was suddenly flanked by high-rise tower blocks and graffiti-scrawled buildings that had seen better days. I turned round and parked in a quiet, pleasant side street which looked a safer option. I made a note of the name of the street – Rue Molière: it would be easy to remember as I knew Molière was a famous French playwright. I was about a mile from the famous old velodrome where the race would finish. I unfolded my trusty Brompton and followed the crowds. I had my phone and knew I could easily get back to Rue Molière using Google Maps after the race.

A stream of fans made towards the velodrome and barriers clearly showed the race route. The crowds lined the roads and I carried on towards the finish. Locking the bike to a post at the velodrome entrance, I made my way into the stadium. Entry was free and the stands were full of excited spectators who had been waiting all day, watching the race unfold on giant screens. The scene took my breath away. I had watched this race on television many times, my copy of *Sunday in Hell* was worn by repeated plays, and here I was: watching John Degenkolb take a famous win in front of a roaring crowd.

I'd had a great day. I'd seen the race half a dozen times, at the start and finish, and was keen to get back on the road to my hotel in Saint-Omer to relax with a few Leffes and a giant steak. I jumped on the Brompton, ready to retrace my steps back to the car. Unfortunately, it wasn't that simple. This was when one of the best days of my life became my worst day.

Everything looked different without the barriers, post-race. I put 'Rue Molière' into Google Maps and it took me somewhere unrecognisable. I had never been here before. Nothing was familiar. I spent the next two hours riding around on my bike, unable to find my car. It got darker and colder, and I was dressed in a T-shirt. Since the discovery of blood clots in my lungs a few years earlier, I took Warfarin pills every day to thin my blood and prevent a dangerous repeat. Worryingly, my medication was in my car, and my phone battery was dead. I was getting increasingly desperate, and retraced my steps to the velodrome four times. Roubaix is a rough town and there I was: a large ginger tourist riding around on a folding bike, looking like a gorilla doing tricks in a circus ring. I was lost, completely panicked, cycling around various housing estates with gangs staring at me from street corners. Quite frantic, I rode back to the velodrome, which was by now deserted, and persuaded a young security guard to call me a taxi.

An hour later, the taxi arrived. He asked where I wanted to go and I explained my situation. He shrugged. I had to give him an address. I told him Rue Molière and he took me back to that unfamiliar place in the middle of the estates. Despite his protestations, I begged him to keep driving till we found my car.

I spent a further two hours in the taxi roaming the streets, with a driver from Lille who had never been to Roubaix. He spoke no English. We retraced my steps several times, and I was panicking before sinking into despondency. We were both getting desperate and hopelessly frustrated, with tempers fraying. I was imagining the humiliation of the press campaign that would try to help me find my car the next day.

Incredibly, as we were finally giving up and looking for a hotel where I could stay, the driver suggested one more route – one that seemed illogical, but it was the only road we hadn't driven that evening. As soon as we left the motorway, I recognised something. I had seen that shopfront before. The area was familiar – it all came flooding back, and then suddenly, we came across my car. The taxi cost me €120, but I would happily have paid double. I can't even begin to contemplate what would have happened without that outrageous piece of luck. I kissed the driver.

The car was, as I had thought, in Rue Molière, and I was at a loss as to why I hadn't found it earlier. I arrived at my hotel at midnight and managed to find the last bistro in Saint-Omer that would serve me a pizza and beer. Still confused, once my phone had charged sufficiently, I scoured Google Maps for some clues about Rue Molière. Unbelievably, I found four different Rue Molières in Roubaix, and my particular road wasn't even listed. I discovered later that Roubaix is a suburb of Lille, and my car was parked in a different suburb called Croix, under a mile away. Pre-race diversions had sent me the long way round the town.

So bad memories of Roubaix for me, and mixed feelings for Geraint Thomas too, I would imagine. He had signalled his potential with a win at the junior edition of the Paris-Roubaix race in 2004, and taken one of Sky's best early results with a second-place finish at Arenberg in the 2010 Tour. But he had also suffered some bad luck here. In April 2018 he had withdrawn after a crash on the very first sector of the Paris-Roubaix race. His aim at the Tour de France would be to stay upright across the cobbles and navigate a safe passage to the finish.

Team Sky had made special preparations in 2018. They would use Pinarello K10 bikes, with automatic rear suspension. Over 50 helpers would be placed at the side of the road with spare wheels, in case of accidents. Thomas didn't need those helpers, but others weren't so lucky, as the inevitable crashes affected the day's racing. Richie Porte, one of the pre-race favourites, was forced to abandon the 2018 Tour after hitting the road just 10 km into the stage. Froome, Landa and Urán also went down as John Degenkolb repeated his 2015 Roubaix win.

It was fascinating to watch as Geraint demonstrated the maturity and discipline needed by a Grand Tour winner. Instinctively tempted to follow the decisive attack when it went, he instead reigned in his enthusiasm to preserve energy for a long three-week race, as he explained:

> It's a weird one. In Paris-Roubaix everyone races for the win but in this you've got teammates who don't want to ride because they've got GC guys behind. When the three guys went, I was maybe six or seventh wheel and I thought 'Maybe I could go,' but I decided to wait. Maybe if I'd gone, though, everyone would have followed anyway.

16 July – Rest day

Welsh cycling before Sky

GERAINT THOMAS'S WELSH-SPEAKING father hails from Bancyfelin, a small village near Carmarthen in west Wales with a history of producing famous rugby players, including Mike Phillips, Delme Thomas and Jonathan Davies. The area also plays a large part in the history of Welsh cycling. Carmarthen's cycle track was opened in 1900, and claims to be the oldest velodrome in continuous use in the world. It joined other Victorian cycling venues in Wales such as Merthyr's Penydarren Park, the People's Park in Llanelli, and St Helen's and the Vetch Fields in Swansea. There were also tracks at the Harlequins Ground, Alexandra Park and Sophia Gardens in Cardiff. Thousands would cram into the grounds and watch outdoor racing. The sport became so popular by the early twentieth century that professional circuits were developed at Taff Vale Park in Pontypridd and at the Ynys Fields in Aberdare. It was in Aberdare that a quartet of world-famous cyclists put Wales on the map over a century before Geraint Thomas was born. Those men were Jimmy Michael and three brothers: Arthur, Samuel and Tom Linton.

Aberdare Cycling Club was formed in 1884, joining other clubs like Cardiff Jockeys and my old friends, the 100 Milers. The Linton family had moved to Aberaman from Somerset in search of work when Arthur was only three, and in 1891 there is a record of Samuel Linton being arrested for 'fierce riding' in Aberdare Park. Samuel was Arthur's younger brother, intent on following in his elder brother's footsteps before a successful career was curtailed by injury. Although Arthur Linton was actually born in England (as Arthur Lenton), he always considered himself Welsh, even riding with three feathers on his chest. Arthur entered one of his first races at Cardiff Harlequins rugby ground, and in 1893 recorded 22 miles, 150 yards in an hour on that track, though as his effort was paced, it was not recognised officially as a world record. But it was enough to persuade the young miner to turn professional.

Linton travelled to Paris that year with his new coach, a controversial character called Choppy Warburton. In his first year in Paris he won several notable races, breaking more world records in front of crowds of up to 20,000. Known unofficially as 'Champion Cyclist of the World', Arthur Linton was soon a star in Paris, competing in the biggest races of the day. He was fourth in the 1896 Paris-Roubaix and then came his greatest achievement, a win in the Bordeaux-Paris race later that year. After winning that race, ill health forced Linton home to Wales, where he died of typhoid six weeks later, aged just 28 years old. A blue plaque has been erected on his house in Aberdare.

Linton had been friendly in Aberdare with a young cyclist called Jimmy Michael, and there are reports that he had lent him his first racing bike. Like so many old cyclists, Michael had been employed (by his parents) as a butcher's boy, delivering meat and running errands on his bike. Jimmy Michael stood at just over five foot, weighing seven stone, in stark contrast to the bigger, more powerful riders of his day. At a Herne Hill race in 1894, he broke the 50 mile record, and earned an invitation to race in Paris, the world centre of track cycling. Then in 1895, Jimmy Michael and Linton's brother Tom joined Arthur as professionals in Choppy Warburton's Gladiator team. At Velodrome Buffalo, Jimmy Michael became the first person to ride 100 miles in under four hours. Michael went further afield, winning races across Europe, in Germany and Belgium. In 1895 he became World Champion after winning a race in Cologne. Jimmy Michael was so famous that he was sketched by the world-renowned painter Toulouse-Lautrec.

Publicised as 'The Champion of the World', Arthur Linton's boasting irritated his old friend. Michael published a challenge to race both him and his brother Tom and insisted that it was he, not Linton, who was the true World Champion. After Linton's death, Michael went to America, where he would race against Tom Linton. After one disastrous race, he accused his own coach, Choppy Warburton, of poisoning him to ensure that he would lose. Warburton was banned from tracks by the National Cyclists' Union in 1896 after a witness saw him give Michael a drink from a small bottle just prior to a race, with Michael then losing his speed, his form, and sometimes finding it difficult to steer his bike in a straight line. Gambling away his money and turning to drink after a heavy crash left him in constant pain, Jimmy Michael died of delirium tremens in 1904 aged just 27, while sailing to race in America. With both Jimmy Michael and Arthur Linton dying before they reached 30 and Tom Linton before he reached 40, questions have been asked about Warburton's connections with the young cyclists.

Born less than a decade after Jimmy Michael's death, Reg Braddick would became a name synonymous with cycling in Cardiff. Like Michael (and Fausto Coppi), Braddick had also been a butcher's boy before starting racing. In 1938 he represented Wales at the Empire Games in Sydney, making the arduous journey by boat. Frustrated by training on rollers, he left the ship as it entered the Suez Canal and raced the 120 miles to the end, having to wait some time for the cruiser to arrive. Six years later he won the British Road Race Championships, before opening his cycle shop on Broadway, Roath. Braddick formed the Cardiff Ajax Cycling Club in 1948 and was a familiar face to Cardiff cyclists until his death in 1999.

One famous member of that Cardiff Ajax Club was Sally Hodge, who would become a World Champion on the track, winning the points race in 1988. Hodge was a double Olympian and took bronze in the 1994 Commonwealth Games. Another rider, Nicole Cooke, is arguably Wales' greatest sportswoman, and indisputably our best cyclist before Geraint Thomas. Cooke's family were all members of Ajax, and aged just 16 she stunned everybody by winning the British Road Race Championship, becoming the youngest ever winner. After a stunning season in 2001 during which she won British titles and four Junior World titles in different disciplines, Cooke turned professional in 2002.

Wins followed at the Commonwealth Games (2002), the Women's World Cup (2003, 2006), the Women's Grand Boucle (2006, 2007) and the Giro d'Italia (2004). Cooke went on to win the British Championship Road Race ten times, and became World Road Race Champion in 2008. That same year, Nicole Cooke took her most stunning victory in the Beijing Olympics. It was one of the most amazing cycling performances that I'd ever witnessed, and the emotional moment when she raised her arms in the rain at the finish was one to treasure.

When Geraint Thomas started the 2007 Tour de France, he became only the second Welsh rider to take part in the race. The first was Colin Lewis, who was born in Abertysswg in 1942. Lewis spent his early years in south Wales before his family moved to Devon when he was still a boy. With legs strengthened by a youth spent riding the Devon hills delivering newspapers, Lewis joined his local cycling club and began winning races. In 1964, he was selected to represent Great Britain in the 1964 Tokyo Olympics. After moving to Brittany to join the Vannes club, Lewis then joined Mackeson-Condor where he was selected to ride the 1967 Tour. On that race, he rode in support of Tom Simpson and shared a room with the Englishman before he tragically died on the climb of the Ventoux. Lewis would ride the Tour again in 1968, when he also won the British Road Race Championship for the second successive year.

STAGE 10

Annecy to
Le Grand-Bornand

THE ROUTE FOR Stage 10 would skirt the town of Cluses, the location of my very first visit to the Tour in 1994. My first visit to the Alps was also my first visit to the Tour *in* France. I had been to a pretty dull stage in Portsmouth earlier in the 1994 Tour, but it was enough to make me want to experience the race in its natural setting. I decided just a few days before the race reached the Alps that I was going to set out on an adventure. Before the days of budget air travel, flights were not as easy to come by as they are now. I booked a flight from Cardiff to Paris, with the intention of catching a train to Geneva, and on to Cluses for the end of Stage 18 and the start of Stage 19 the following day. It didn't work out quite as I'd planned.

The Cardiff to Paris flight was not well used. The aeroplane was tiny with maybe 20 seats, similar to the domestic flight that now links Cardiff to Anglesey. And on 20th July 1994, there were only half a dozen passengers aboard, one of whom was a very pretty girl from Swansea. We began chatting and

I discovered that she had recently split from her boyfriend and was taking a solo trip to Paris to mend her broken heart. I sensed an opportunity and made my move at the baggage reclaim conveyor. Did she know Paris at all, I asked her? Because, as it happened, I was familiar with the City of Love, and believe it or not, I would be passing her hotel on my way to the Gare de Lyon. I could show her around if she liked. That's me all over – I'm such a considerate man.

We took the Métro and got off at Châtelet, in the centre of town. I'd forgotten to mention to my new friend that I'd spent two weeks working at the Théâtre du Châtelet just a short time before our visit. During my time there, I had spent every night in a bistro on the corner of Rue Saint-Denis, and of course I'd become very friendly with the owners. I'm ashamed to admit that I manipulated the situation to my benefit. We left the underground and I casually suggested that we take a break and grab a beer. We strolled along the Rue Saint-Denis and found ourselves outside my regular haunt. "Oh, what about this place?" I suggested nonchalantly. "It looks perfect."

We entered my favourite Parisian drinking place to be greeted by Monsieur Le Patron. "PHILIPPE!" he exclaimed. "It's so good to see you again!" And out came Madame, planting two red lipstick marks on my blushing cheeks. I looked at my Swansea friend and shrugged. "This sort of thing happens to me all the time." I could tell she was impressed. I had a great idea. I could book a room at her hotel, and we could go out for dinner that evening. She agreed with a glint in her eye and I knew that I had made one of the most successful moves in the history of the game. Move over Casanova.

My date began crying before the arrival of the *cuisses de grenouille*. By the time we arrived at the main course, she was inconsolable. "I should never have left him," she wept. Spending time in my company had apparently made her realise just how much she missed him. She left her ice cream to go and call him and tell him what a terrible mistake she'd made. I sat alone at our table in the fancy restaurant, finished the wine and paid the bill. I had missed my train to Geneva for nothing. I gave her room a quick drunken knock when I returned from my lonely Parisian pub crawl, but to no avail. "Go away," she shouted.

I left early the next morning without saying goodbye and jumped on the train to Geneva. I knew there was a line to Cluses but I hadn't realised it was the Alpine equivalent of the steam train from Porthmadog to Blaenau Ffestiniog. In what seemed like a never-ending journey, my connection made its lazy way through beautiful *Sound of Music* scenery and finally approached the finish town. I arrived in Cluses about 40 minutes after the end of the stage, just as everybody was leaving. I was like a salmon swimming upstream as I battled against the crowds making their way home. It felt like I was walking around IKEA the wrong way. Despondently regretting my Parisian liaison, I vowed never again to let romance interfere with sport and strolled around the finish-line area. I had been wandering aimlessly for a few minutes when I came across some motorhomes decorated with team logos. I walked towards them and stopped suddenly when I noticed a small man sitting on the steps of one of the vans. It was only flipping Marco Pantani!

My hero looked at me and I looked at him. He had obviously noticed my jaw dropping to the floor and the grin spreading across my chubby cheeks. "Marco, M-Marco..." I stuttered. He gazed towards me with barely concealed contempt, waiting for my next sentence. But that was all I had. I knew not a word of Italian, so I just gestured towards his cap and suggested in international finger-pointing sign language that he gave it to me as a souvenir. *"Vaffanculo!"* he responded.

I complied with Mr Pantani's request and went off to look for the local tourist office. I hadn't booked any accommodation but I was sure that it wouldn't be a problem. Yes, I was that naive, but there was no booking.com or airbnb in those days. And yes, of course it was a problem. With no accommodation available, I decided to hitch-hike the 25 miles to Morzine to find a room. Looking back now, it seems like a disastrous trip on all fronts, but I don't remember being concerned at all. And when I climbed up into the cab of a lorry which was heading to my destination, I was feeling pretty pleased with myself. An hour later, as darkness approached, I sauntered confidently up to the window of the Morzine Tourist Office. I saw a notice taped to the window of the office, which was of course, closed.

> All accommodation full. Emergency shelter available at the local school.

I shared my first night's sleep at the Tour de France with a dozen other intrepid, disorganised travellers in Morzine's school hall. We slept on gym mattresses covered with old blankets and rose at dawn to find a spot on the mountain for that day's stage. I watched the sun rise across Alpine peaks as I humped a rucksack full of sandwiches and beer on a two-hour hike along the route of the mountain time trial. I sat in the shade alongside a happy crew of Spanish families who were singing songs and generally having a good time. I discovered that time trials were exciting for a while as riders passed at two-minute intervals, including the Tashkent Terror, Djamolidine Abdoujaparov, but it was easy to get bored by the procession until the big names arrived at the end of the day. There was Tonkov, Pantani, then his polka-dotted rival Virenque, who I despised even then. And finally came Miguel Induráin, the world's most boring cyclist, wearing his yellow jersey. My companions from Asturias went crazy.

I managed to find a bus service that took me to Geneva, where I stayed at a hotel next to the lake. The next day I caught the train for a short journey to Annemasse, a nondescript town where I watched the *peloton* pass in rain jackets before making my way back to Paris. Compared to later trips, this first one was uninspiring in hindsight, but I had met Marco Pantani and learnt a lot about the logistics of watching the Tour that would stand me in good stead.

Stage 10 of the 2018 Tour would start in Annecy, some 25 miles south of Annemasse. I had chosen the 'Venice of the Alps' as my base for the Tour three years earlier. It's a stunning location and we had camped at the southern end of the lake at Doussard, about 10 miles south of the city, along the best cycle path I've ever ridden in my life. The 2018 route circuited the lake and went through Doussard before climbing the Col de Bluffy to Thomes. The lake is surrounded by steepish hills which are great for climbing and other activities. My kids went hang-gliding from the top back to Doussard, while I cycled down. If you want to follow the Tour as a family, Annecy is an ideal place to combine sport with a holiday.

In 2018, this was the first chance for us to see how Thomas would climb in the Tour. He had never been so trim. Thomas's weight was officially announced as 10 st 9 lb, though he looked lighter when I saw him in Pau towards the end of the race. We didn't get to see much action as the top riders were keeping their powder dry for the difficult days to follow. There was a sombre moment as riders slowed to pay their respects at Glières Plateau, where resistance soldiers were killed during a World War II battle. The gravel road on the plateau caused some dramatic dust clouds, creating scenes that reminded the viewer of the Strade Bianche race, which runs over white dirt roads in Tuscany.

It was Luke Rowe who led the *peloton* up to the Plateau, and then he kept going at the front for almost 100 kilometres, until the foot of the Col de Romme. It was an epic performance from Rowe, who had not even expected to be at the race after a terrible accident ten months earlier. In August 2017, he had shattered his leg in over 20 places when he jumped into shallow water during his brother's stag party in Prague. He wasn't even drunk – the accident happened in the morning during a white-water rafting session. He was told by a surgeon that he might never ride again but Rowe battled back to fitness, encouraged by messages of support – including one from international footballer Aaron Ramsey, who had himself recovered from a broken leg. He hadn't expected to be fit to ride the Tour and had set a vague target of making the Vuelta in September.

Speaking to *The Telegraph*'s Tom Cary, he explained how the crash could still affect his career, running a finger up and down his lower leg, where he has a metal rod:

> We've had a few discussions about whether to leave it in or take it out. And we've decided that we're going to leave it in; to strengthen the tibia. But if I was to crash and if it was a big one, well, you can imagine… the rod bends, the bone doesn't. So it would shatter and I would never ride a bike again. Potentially never walk again. I would never have full use of my leg.

But here he was at the Tour de France in 2018, and not just riding it but eating up the miles at the front of the *peloton*. The prize money for winning the Tour is €500,000, which is traditionally shared out between team riders and staff – but not the winner, who is rewarded in other ways with sponsorships and appearances. Luke Rowe earned his share of the prize money on this and several other stages during the Tour. He told *BBC Wales Sport*:

> It is still quite strange sometimes when you think about the whole story with me and Geraint, in how long ago it was that we were two little kids racing around with Maindy Flyers. Messing around on the street on our BMXs together and we've kind of slowly but surely gone through the ranks together. He is three or four years older than me so he was always that one step ahead. To go through the ranks together and see each other progressing and bounce off each other a bit, to now be going year-on-year to the Tour de France, the biggest bike race in the world, together… Just two Cardiff lads bombing around Maindy causing carnage, to going to the best bike race in the world and being successful. It is a pretty cool story.

Unlike Geraint Thomas, Luke Rowe comes from a strong cycling background. His father Courtney is a cycling coach, and I came across another member of the family at Saint-Jean-de-Maurienne during the Tour a few years ago. I had been waiting with my wife at the roadside on a steep climb out of the small town when we spotted a Welsh flag on the opposite side of the road. It was being carried by a tall, slim man wearing full cycling kit and no shoes. We exchanged greetings and started chatting about the race.

We discovered that our compatriot was there to see his brother, who he was expecting to arrive soon. As the race approached, he was still alone on the roadside and we sympathised that his brother hadn't made it. Then about 20 minutes after Vincenzo Nibali had gone through on his way to victory, we saw Luke Rowe approaching with a beaming grin on his face. He raised his hand and shared a fist-bump with our new friend. "Come on, bro!" he shouted, as I took the best photograph of my life. I'd just seen Luke Rowe meet his brother, while riding his first Tour de France. I've since learnt that Matt Rowe is a former European Champion cyclist who runs a cycle coaching business with his wife Dani (née King), herself an Olympic medallist in team pursuit who now represents Wales.

One of Luke Rowe's former teammates, Bradley Wiggins, had used the rest day to raise the Team Sky leadership question on his podcast. He had been involved with his own leadership tussle with Chris Froome in 2012 and was direct in his assessment of Dave Brailsford's likely approach to the current situation:

He's quite self-serving. For him it's about the team winning, it's not about the individuals or the characters. He will always be in those riders' ears constantly, and he has been up till now, as you can see. Both riders have got this joint leadership role, but that's dangerous.

Dave will certainly get in both of their ears and be telling them they can both win it, as a way of motivating them, a way of playing these cards deep into the race and let the natural selection come into play. If Geraint stays where he is and takes the yellow jersey, they've got a real problem on their hands.

Thomas did stay where he was, looking comfortable on the climbs, but he did not take yellow.

Alaphilippe took the stage and Greg Van Avermaet fought like a tiger to keep the yellow jersey for another precious day. Team Sky were content to let the Belgian increase his lead on Thomas as they knew he was not a long-term danger and were in no hurry to take a jersey that they would have to defend.

STAGE 11

Albertville to La Rosière

THE CRITÉRIUM DU Dauphiné is an 8-day stage race which was first contested in 1947. Historically, it has been used for preparation for the Tour de France, and is seen as a good indication of form ahead of the bigger race. Recent Dauphiné/ Tour double winners have included Chris Froome and Bradley Wiggins, and many of the sport's legendary names have also won both in the same year. Louison Bobet did it in 1955; Jacques Anquetil in 1963; Eddy Merckx in 1971; Luis Ocaña in 1973; Bernard Thévenet in 1975; Bernard Hinault in 1979 and 1981, and Miguel Induráin in 1995. Lance Armstrong won the race in 2002 and 2003 (though he was stripped of the titles in the wake of the doping scandal). Geraint Thomas's inclusion in the 2018 Dauphiné for Team Sky was significant.

With Chris Froome rested after riding the Giro d'Italia, Team Sky announced that leadership at the Dauphiné would be shared between Thomas and Pole Michał Kwiatkowski, who had both returned from intensive training at a high-altitude camp in Tenerife. Thomas didn't enjoy these camps, as he admitted to *The Times*'s Mathew Syed in 2016:

It's a tough way to live but the deeper we go here, the better
our prospects. You have just got to keep that in your head,
particularly when you are low on fuel. Otherwise you might go
fucking bonkers.

When Kwiatkowski won the Dauphiné Prologue, while Thomas
crashed, he seemed to be the man in pole position to lead the
team. But when the race went into the mountains on Stage 4,
Kwiatkowski was soon dropped while Thomas took the yellow
jersey after a strong performance to finish second behind Dan
Martin on Stage 5. Stage 6 of the Dauphiné involved scaling
four mountains – the Montée de Bisanne, the Col du Pré and
the Cormet de Roselend, finishing with the final climb to the
ski resort of La Rosière – the exact route that would feature on
Stage 11 of the Tour de France in July.

That Dauphiné stage to La Rosière was a short course of
only 110 km, but that kind of day had been proven to rip races
apart as riders felt readier to attack without fear of blowing
up late on. Romain Bardet's AG2R team rode aggressively to
disrupt Sky on the Col du Pré and with Pello Bilbao riding clear
at the head of the race, Thomas was left without teammates
in a group of four potential Tour de France rivals – Thomas,
Romain Bardet, Adam Yates, and Dan Martin. With 350 m
remaining, Thomas sprinted away from the group to land a
psychological blow and gain a few more seconds in the race
for the Dauphiné overall. Bardet gave his view on Thomas's
performance:

Honestly, there was nothing I could do against him today. He
has such a big lead that he can just manage things, and he was
the strongest in the finale today. When we come to the slightly

gentler gradients, being a former track rider, he can really dish out the pain.

Despite two punctures on the final stage, Thomas took the overall win with a measured effort. Speaking to *The Cycling Podcast*, Sky's Tao Geoghegan Hart said he felt that Thomas had another gear left and hadn't really extended himself to win the race. This boded well for the forthcoming Tour.

The competition would be a little stronger when the Tour de France revisited the stage, but Thomas would be confident of his chances. And when the day came, the race played out in an uncannily similar repeat of the Dauphiné stage a month earlier. This time, instead of Pello Bilbao, it was former Sky rider Mikel Nieve who was up the road on his own, followed by Tom Dumoulin, who had attacked on the penultimate descent. With 5 km left, Sky's final *domestique*, Michał Kwiatkowski, came to a halt after leading the team up the final climb and Thomas set off in pursuit of Dumoulin. The big question was whether Froome would let him go. And he did, seemingly goading the other contenders to chase down the Welshman until Martin took on the challenge. Thomas soon joined Dumoulin and Damiano Caruso in a small group of three behind Nieve. This was playing out just like the Dauphiné.

With just a kilometre to go, it looked like Nieve would take the stage in the same way Bilbao had taken it in June. Thomas was sitting on Dumoulin's wheel in the same way that he had sat on others' wheels in the Dauphiné. And he repeated the same attack, starting it a few hundred metres earlier this time. The gentle gradient that Bardet had spoken about allowed Thomas to leave Dumoulin in his wake as he chased down Nieve. I don't think anybody expected him to catch his former teammate, but he was making vital time on his rivals – including, crucially, Chris Froome. Then, dramatically, Thomas flew past the stunned Nieve with 350 m to the line – the exact place where he had begun his Dauphiné attack. He could sprint to the line with confidence. Nieve was a spent force.

Geraint Thomas had sent out a strong message and put himself forward as a serious contender for the Tour de France. His win was greeted with a mixture of cheers and jeers, the only disappointment after a stunning performance which Geraint called "one of the best days of my career". Froome came in strongly to finish 20 seconds behind Thomas, but his Sky leadership was now in doubt with a gap of 1:25 to his teammate. Dumoulin was third overall at 1:44 but nobody else was within two minutes of Thomas, who held a healthy lead at this stage of the race.

"It is unreal and I didn't expect it at all," Thomas said as he took the yellow jersey for the second day. He was almost apologetic about stealing the win from his former colleague. "I could see Mikel, and it's a shame, but I had to go for that win because it was super nice."

Phil on the
Champs-Élysées,
1994

Miguel Induráin at
Annemasse, 1994

Phil offers a
helping hand on
the Galibier, 1998

Jan Ullrich loses the Tour, 1998

Tom Simpson memorial, Mont Ventoux

Phil and his flag greet Marco Pantani on the summit of the Col du Galibier 1998

Phil and Tommie Collins, Argelès-Gazost, 2012

Phil and Tommie at the summit of the Tourmalet, 2012

Waiting for the Tour on the Alpe d'Huez, 2013

Alpe d'Huez, 2013

Start of the 2014 Tour at Harewood House, Yorkshire

2014 Tour de France, Yorkshire

Alpe d'Huez summit

A cheeky selfie with Chris Boardman, Bagnères-de-Luchon, 2014

Col de Peyresourde, 2014

Bagnères-de-Luchon, 2014

Excitement as the caravan arrives, 2014

Col des Bordères, 2014

An inflatable alien Geraint Thomas

Riding the Paris-Roubaix cobbles on a Brompton

Geraint Thomas, Compiègne, 2015

Geraint Thomas, Trouée d'Arenberg, 2015

Roubaix Velodrome, 2015

Matt Rowe meets Luke Rowe riding his first Tour de France, 2015

Col du Glandon on my trusty Orange MTB, 2015

Waving the flag at the Muro di Sormano, Il Lombardia, 2015

Geraint Thomas finishes Stage 18 at Pau

(© Gruff Stead)

Yellow jersey presentation, Pau, 2018

Stage 19, Col du Soulor, 2018

Welsh fans wait for their hero, 2018

Arwyn Thomas, who went to almost every stage of the Tour in 2018

The mist rolls in –
Col du Soulor
(© Scott Thomas)

Pre-tour parade,
Col du Soulor

Thomas climbs to victory on Col de Soulor

Not everybody was friendly – a Spanish supporter shows his feelings

New flag for the Champion – all ready to cheer Geraint home

Thomas arrives at the finish line, Espelette
(© Scott Thomas)

Geraint is welcomed by his wife, Sara, at Espelette
(© Scott Thomas)

Welsh celebrations – Phil, Scott and Rich celebrate a Welsh Champion

Gruff waves from his vantage point above the crowds

Crowd cheers as Geraint takes the yellow jersey
(© Gruff Stead)

The Red Dragon flies as Geraint wins the Tour de France
(© Gruff Stead)

"I've won the
Tour, man"
(© Scott Thomas)

Lapping the
Champs-Élysées
(© Scott Thomas)

Geraint is mobbed
after the final
stage in Paris
(© Scott Thomas)

Geraint and Sara
in Paris
(© Scott Thomas)

A Welsh winner on
the Champs-Élysées
(© Scott Thomas)

Bourg-Saint-Maurice to Alpe d'Huez

I WATCHED STAGE 12 as-live, several hours after it had taken place. I often try to avoid hearing the stage result until I arrive home from work, but I rarely manage it. We have a large television in the kitchen at our offices and my colleagues are usually keen to discuss the race with me. Twitter flashes up notifications and any major incident is reported on the radio as I drive home. But today I went into total lockdown, turning off my phone and leaving the office with my hands over my ears, singing "I'm not listening!" I succeeded in blocking out the world, and was looking forward to four hours of uninterrupted viewing.

The stage began from Bourg-Saint-Maurice and first climbed the Col de la Madeleine before Dutch rider Steven Kruijswijk launched a solo attack up the Col de la Croix de Fer, crossing the summit with a six-minute lead over the *peloton*. The Croix de Fer is one of my favourite climbs, with its peak just across from the Col du Glandon. When the race passes west from St Jean de Maurienne, it's possible to access the summit from the northern side by climbing the Glandon from the village of St-Étienne-de-Cuines. In 2015, I was out of shape and left early to drive this route to watch the race on the Croix de Fer. No such luck. Arriving early in the morning, several hours before the race was due to pass, *gendarmes* were already barring the way. I hadn't expected this, and was left with little choice. Wearing baggy shorts and an ironic 'Pédaleur de Charme' T-shirt, I was forced to try to ride up on my 20-year-old old banger of a mountain bike with its broken gears. Too many hours later, having limped up the last steep, morale-sapping hairpin, I arrived at the Glandon/Croix de Fer junction less than 30 minutes before the first riders passed. I had a long history with that old banger – my Orange C16R mountain bike. I had proposed to my girlfriend in 1996 and when she deferred her decision due to our less-than-secure finances, I bought the bike in protest. I slept with it in our bedroom as a pointed reminder of my wealth and petulance. I also thought it rather beautiful, and have never been able to find a better replacement – for either the bike or the girlfriend, who is now my wife.

In 2018, after cresting the Croix de Fer, Steven Kruijswijk glided down one of the most beautiful descents in the Alps, past the stunning Lac de Grand Maison and down into the village of Bourg d'Oisans, before taking on the legendary Alpe d'Huez. He was going for broke and had spoken about winning alone on the Alpe.

The Alpe d'Huez is cycling's most iconic climb. It is the Wembley, the Wimbledon, the Cardiff Arms Park of cycling.

First included in 1952, it has been the scene of some of the Tour's most memorable moments. When Fausto Coppi won at the Alpe in front of live cameras on the Tour's first summit finish, its reputation as the Hollywood climb was established immediately. At the same place in 1986, teammates Greg LeMond and Bernard Hinault joined hands to cross the line, giving us some of the most famous images of the race. After my illness, I made it a target to climb the Alpe d'Huez. I could have chosen any number of climbs, but this was the one I had dreamed about when lying on the hospital bed. If I got better, I would climb the Alpe. I had heard that a local route – the climb from Llanberis up to Deiniolen and again to Marchlyn Mawr reservoir – was a similar gradient, apparently replicating a third of the Alpe d'Huez almost exactly. I rode it a few times in preparation, even though I was sceptical about any similarities.

I made my Alpe d'Huez attempt in 2013, a day before the Tour arrived. The road rises immediately from Bourg d'Oisans with no warning or warm-up slope. I would say that the shock of this and the realisation that there are 13 more kilometres of climbing makes the earliest part the most difficult. Once you settle down into a rhythm on the 8% average, it isn't so fearsome. And it was true, the road was uncannily reminiscent of that climb to Marchlyn Mawr.

Each of the hairpin bends on the Alpe d'Huez feature the names of stage winners. All the bends were full by 2001, so Lance Armstrong's name was added next to Coppi's at Switchback 21, the first turn at the bottom. I read them all as I passed. Here I was, riding in the same arena as Coppi,

Zoetemelk, Hinault, and my hero, Pantani. Happy spectators cheered me on as I struggled up the climb in my Clwb Beicio Menai jersey and red dragon socks. *"Allez, allez! Courage! Bravo, pays de Galles!"* I really wish I could say that it was awesome. And of course, it was a great experience. But the Alpe d'Huez is one of the uglier climbs in the Alps, and I much preferred others that I had ridden. The summit itself is marked only by a small lamp post and I rode past for a few kilometres looking for something more significant amongst the high-rise apartment blocks. There was nothing – that unremarkable sign was the only indicator. There are much more beautiful climbs in the area, but of course, if you're there, you have to ride it. It's another one for the bucket list.

In 2013, I stood on the road to watch the Tour come past twice as it repeated the climb at the end of the stage. Shouting for Geraint Thomas, with my son waving a large Welsh flag, he lifted a finger off the bars in recognition as he passed in a large, fully focussed group. Fair play, I thought, he's climbing the Alpe d'Huez in the Tour de France, and still has time to acknowledge his Welsh fans. One of the reasons the Alpe d'Huez attracts so many fans is that access to the summit is unmatched. On race day, it's possible to walk straight up from Bourg d'Oisans, take a cable car from the village of Oz, or (like we did) stay for the night at Villard Reculas with an easy walk across to the finish line. Visitors and locals streamed from the village across to the route in a colourful procession of families, cyclists and tourists. We knew that we were getting close as we began to hear the loud beats of the booming DJ sound system, mixed with chanting from the thousands of fans at

Dutch Corner. It felt as though we were walking to the biggest Alpine party that ever was. And in a sense, we were.

The Alpe is sometimes known as 'The Dutch Mountain', due to a series of Dutch winners at the climb in the late 1970s. Switchback 7,near the Église Saint-Ferréol became a popular gathering place for cycling fans from the Netherlands. The area was sanitised for the 2018 race, with rope barriers at the side of the road and alcohol-free beer on sale at the makeshift bar. While traditionalists complained about the loss of spectacle, it was inevitable after the recent escalation in crowd interference.

I went to sample the atmosphere in 2015, when Dutch Corner was at its most chaotic. Maybe I'm getting a bit old for all this, but it seemed to be another 'look at me!' location where people are desperate to be noticed as they dance on the roads in fancy dress. Decked out in orange, the boozy crowd have now added flares to their repertoire, creating a thick fog which fills the riders' lungs and reduces vision to a few metres. I wasn't sorry when restrictions were put in place this year, but the Dutch still went crazy when their man Kruijswijk began the climb. He had reached Alpe d'Huez with over 4 minutes' lead on the yellow-jersey group, which included the young Colombian, Egan Bernal. This was the day Bernal came of age, firstly by setting a blistering pace at the foot of the climb and then covering attacks by Nibali and Quintana before handing over responsibilities to Thomas, who by following attacks by Landa and Bardet seemed to be at least sharing responsibility with Froome. A group of Welsh fans, including riders from Energy Cycling Club, had designated Bend 14 as Welsh Corner. A huge banner of Geraint Thomas in his Wales kit was pinned to the back wall and Welsh flags were joined by Union Jacks as other Brits looked to join in the party.

Dramatically, Nibali went down in the chaos of the race and Thomas was forced to ride over his back wheel. The Italian had been crowded out by motorbikes and encroaching fans, and his bars caught the swinging strap of a camera. Thomas could so easily have crashed too, but 2018 was the Tour when his bad luck was replaced by good fortune. The leaders slowed to wait a while for Nibali after his misfortune, and he remounted to bravely ride home, even with a fractured vertebra. But his race was gone.

In what appeared to be the decisive moment, Froome attacked with 3 km to go. He caught and passed Kruijswijk, and I was expecting to see him ride away, taking with him all prospects of a Welsh Tour winner. But Tom Dumoulin refused to concede, and was able to steadily close the gap to Froome, carrying Thomas and Bardet on his wheel. In extraordinary scenes, the four rode side by side across the road, weighing each other up, as Landa was able to rejoin them. If they were waiting for Nibali, then Bardet hadn't read the script. He attacked first, and Froome went too, followed closely by Dumoulin. Events had developed perfectly for Geraint Thomas, as he entered the final having expended less energy than his companions. Thomas selected his race line, and led the five into the final left-hand corner. He was clearly the strongest rider, and I leapt up, punching the air as he rode away for the greatest win in Welsh cycling history. I could not believe what I was seeing. This just does not happen. A Welshman had won on the Alpe d'Huez! Geraint Thomas was dazed:

Honestly, I'm speechless. I don't know what to say. There is not a chance in hell that I thought I was going to win today. I just followed Dumoulin and Bardet while Froome was attacking, and it was bad luck for Nibali. I rode over his back wheel and nearly came down myself.

Can we just go straight to Paris now? I did say yesterday that this race was made for me, and after today, I can be happy. It's one of those things that's going to stay with me for the rest of my life. I'm just going to enjoy it... Alpe d'Huez, man... speechless.

Geraint Thomas climbed Alpe d'Huez with a time of 41:15. That's four and a half minutes slower than Marco Pantani's record and nowhere near the fastest ascents of the climb. Despite the reassuringly average winning time recorded, Thomas was booed by some on the podium as French fans took their frustration out after another win for Team Sky. Froome and Thomas had been spat on, liquid was thrown, arses bared, and one man who had pushed Chris Froome was arrested and handcuffed by police.

In his best, understated Cardiff accent, Thomas pleaded:

Have a bit of decency, like. Boo all you like, but don't affect the race. Don't touch the riders. Don't spit at us. Voice your opinions all you want but let us do the racing.

He went on to claim that his position as a *domestique* remained unaffected by the remarkable win.

I'm still riding for Froomey. Froomey's still our man. He knows how to ride for three weeks.

Yeah, right.

STAGE 13

Bourg d'Oisans
to Valence

VINCENZO NIBALI, ONE of Geraint Thomas's main rivals, was unable to start Stage 13 after scans revealed a broken vertebra from the crash on the Alpe d'Huez. Brent Copeland, manager of Nibali's Bahrain-Merida team, admitted that he was warning his riders to avoid riding with Team Sky:

> In the past we said, 'Guys, stay up front to avoid the crashes'.
> Now we say: 'Don't stay behind Froome: it's dangerous'.

The crowd had been particularly virulent and abusive towards Froome, even though the sale of alcohol had been banned on Dutch Corner. Either beer or some other liquid had been thrown as he rode past. When informed of the incident, Thomas said:

> I'm not surprised. We've had a bit of that. It's always been water from what I've seen. But I wouldn't know what it was.

Stage 13 began at Bourg d'Oisans, the lively village at the foot of the Alpe d'Huez. It's a perfect base for an Alpine cycling holiday, within easy reach of several legendary climbs. We camped at Rochetaillé, which is about 2 km north of the village. It's a good choice when the Tour is in town, but I did feel that we were missing out on some of the great atmosphere that builds up around the race. Walking into town, we saw vans and motorhomes parked on every available piece of land. Even pavements became camping spots and large groups of cyclists sat outside every cafe. Some even risked a beer!

While I was in the area, I set off to ride the Col du Galibier. I had been there on my stag weekend in 1998, driving overnight with three friends crammed into my fiancée's VW Golf. Still a little naive, we spent a big night drinking at our base in Valloire before setting out early, expecting to catch a taxi or a bus to the summit. Of course, we ended up hiking the whole way from the valley to the highest point of the Tour that year. The weather was terrible at the summit, and I was wearing shorts, a T-shirt and a raincoat. It was freezing up there, and we stood for hours in the rain without shelter. I draped myself in my huge Welsh flag and waited for something to happen. Then later that afternoon, with our spirits literally dampened, the Tour arrived. Helicopters buzzed around, we saw the headlamps of a motorcycle come out of the mist, and behind him... who was that? It was Marco Pantani!

The few hardy souls at the summit erupted, I screamed my support and on Eurosport, David Duffield shouted that "the Red Dragon of Wales is looking on as Pantani breathes fire." Then we waited. Nobody came. A long time passed before we saw the yellow jersey of Jan Ullrich. The German was blowing and I knew that we had just witnessed Marco Pantani make the winning move of the 1998 Tour de France. It remains one of the best moments of my life spent watching sport.

Vincenzo Nibali's camera strap-induced crash the previous day on the Alpe d'Huez was typical of several similar accidents in recent years. Crowds have been getting closer and closer to the riders, making these incidents inevitable. Cameras are often the cause of the problems, as I remember well from the dramatic 1994 Tour when unbelievably, a *gendarme* tried to take a photograph from within the barriers of a sprint finish. The crash which occurred when Belgian sprinter Wilf Nelissen hit him at 40 mph led to horrific injuries to several riders.

Giuseppe Guerini was knocked over by a spectator on the Alpe d'Huez as he rode to a stage victory in the 1999 edition of the Tour. With the finishing line in sight, the man stepped into the road to take a photograph and took Guerini out completely. The rider remounted and won the stage nonetheless. In 2014, Andy Schleck needed surgery after colliding with a spectator who moved out into the road to take photographs. At the same tour a crash was caused by a fan who was taking a selfie with their back to the race. The Nibali incident reminded me of Lance Armstrong's crash on the 2003 Tour. Wearing the yellow jersey, Lance Armstrong was climbing Luz Ardiden when he rode too close to the spectators and caught his handlebar on the strap of someone's bag. Jan Ullrich avoided the crash, and took the virtual race lead from Armstrong. But he waited for the American, refusing to take advantage of his misfortune. Armstrong quickly re-mounted his bike and caught Ullrich, going on to win the Tour.

This kind of chivalry is not unusual in cycling – it's

considered unacceptable to capitalise on bad luck, especially if the unfortunate cyclist is wearing yellow. I have to admit finding this frustrating sometimes. If somebody suffers a puncture because they've chosen lighter tyres, or suffer a mechanical because they're trying out an innovative technology, I believe they are responsible. And luck plays a huge part in most sports. I think cycling would be a lot more exciting if we believed that something dramatic could happen at any minute to affect the race. Of course, in the Armstrong incident, a spectator was involved, which set it outside the category of 'misfortune'.

Ullrich should have won that Tour, but instead he behaved according to cycling's unwritten code of honour. It was a magnificent gesture which was soon forgotten by the German public, who disowned Ullrich after his doping was revealed in 2006. Humiliated and shamed, he suffered psychological problems and was arrested twice just days after the 2018 Tour. Meanwhile Richard Virenque, Laurent Jalabert, David Millar and several other confirmed dopers were happily fronting television coverage. Ullrich's only friend seemed to be Lance Armstrong, who has consistently offered support to a rival he greatly respects. Like me, Geraint Thomas was an Ullrich fan, rushing home from school to cheer him on each day.

The day's route from Bourg d'Oisans to Valence offered a welcome respite after the craziness of Alpe d'Huez. Peter Sagan won the sprint after a flattish stage which had not affected the overall race contenders. The only threat to Geraint Thomas's yellow jersey was a lit flare which was thrown near the Team Sky riders with 20 km of the day remaining.

STAGE 14

Saint-Paul-Trois-
Châteaux to Mende

STAGE 14 TRAVERSED some of France's most beautiful, yet for many British visitors least familiar, territory. Starting in the Massif Central, the race crossed the Rhône and headed up the Ardèche gorge. It was difficult, hilly territory which would need to be controlled well by Team Sky.

The Tour had last finished in Mende in 2015, when Geraint Thomas lost almost a minute to Froome. There was speculation that maybe the Welshman would be vulnerable again on the steep climb. But the comparison was superficial, failing to take into account the work that Thomas had been doing in service of his leader three years earlier.

Basque rider Omar Fraile sped into Mende in 2018 to win the stage, and Primož Roglič was the only GC contender to gain time, finishing eight seconds ahead of Thomas, Froome and Dutchman Tom Dumoulin. Dumoulin had made an attempt at an attack in the final kilometres but he was chased down by Thomas, with Froome in tow. When Froome then broke clear,

Thomas and Dumoulin were able to bring him back without too many problems. Of Dumoulin, Thomas said:

> He can really pace himself. You don't know if he is really suffering or just pacing himself. Fair play to do that, it takes some balls to do that, especially when you have no teammates.

Dumoulin is a likeable, open rider who has developed into one of the most consistent racers on the world tour. Like Thomas, and Primož Roglič, he's a *rouleur* who has trained and conditioned himself to climb well. Rarely thrilling, Dumoulin is the epitome of the modern power-meter rider. He's an exceptional athlete who knows his physical limits and rides independently, seemingly unaffected by the race around him. Dumoulin is used to riding alone in the mountains, unable to rely on the strong bevy of teammates that is available to Thomas and Froome. Sitting in third as their biggest challenger, he felt that the battle for leadership at Team Sky might allow him a gap to capitalise on their internal competition.

"It's difficult but they also are riding for their win," he answered, when asked if he could compete with two riders from Sky. He mischievously revealed that it was Thomas who had helped him close down Froome in the final, and indeed, that's how it had looked back in Wales. Thomas was asked whether the Team Sky management had given specific instructions:

> I'm sure they'd be happy for either of us to win. But for me, I'd be happier if I won than Froomey!

So would I, Geraint *bach*. So would I.

Stage 15

Millau to Carcassonne

THREE INTERMEDIATE CLIMBS awaited the riders as the race travelled south-east on its way towards the Pyrenees. It could be a day for the breakaway and Team Sky would need to concentrate fully on managing the day. Geraint Thomas was enjoying his time in yellow, but he was definitely not getting ahead of himself.

> I'm not thinking of winning the Tour de France. I take each day as it comes, just worry about the next stage. The yellow jersey is definitely a confidence booster. It's a massive honour. I'm having the race of my life. In the Pyrenees, it'll be 50% in the legs and 50% in the head. I have to stay strong. What I can do in the third week remains an unknown, but the third week is hard for everyone.

The day's main talking point came when Sky's Gianni Moscon appeared to punch the Fortuneo-Samsic rider Élie Gesbert after just 800 m. The two riders had words, then Moscon looked back and swung his right arm into the face of Gesbert. He was disqualified from the Tour. Team Sky had already shown leniency towards the Italian for two other incidents. He had previously been suspended after making racist comments

94

to rider Kévin Reza, and had been accused of hitting Swiss rider Sébastien Reichenbach. But now Dave Brailsford said that Team Sky supported and accepted his disqualification. It would be a blow to Sky, whose usual nine-rider group had already been reduced to eight by new rules. Losing even one rider would make a race more difficult to control.

The new rule reducing the number of team members was intended to enliven the racing, and I was in favour. I used to hate watching Armstrong's US Postal team control the Tour, and without Thomas and Rowe, I think I'd feel the same about Sky. It may be rose-tinted nostalgia, but racing did feel a lot more unpredictable back in the day. Sky's team has been the strongest at the race for years now, and its multitude of world-class riders are able to ride opponents into submission. They can sit at the front all day and then drive hard into the mountains, keeping up such a relentless pace that it's nearly impossible for an opponent to attack.

Modern technology has dampened down some of the excitement too. Team managers now have television monitors in their cars and are able to watch the race develop. Information is relayed to riders via radio, and power meters calculate the effort required from them throughout the day. It's almost impossible to imagine now that Robert Millar lost 'the stolen Vuelta' in 1985 because he was unaware that his rival, Pedro Delgado, had attacked. Modern teams and riders will insist this is a good thing, of course, but for the viewer, a layer of drama and unpredictability has been removed. Personally, I'd like to see radios and power meters banned from every race.

Thankfully, breakaways are still possible, and Magnus Cort Nielsen took the stage with a second consecutive breakaway win for Astana. Geraint Thomas crossed with Froome and Dumoulin, the GC unaffected. He told BBC Radio 5 Live:

> It is rattling through quite nicely and I am looking forward to the rest day. I am not even thinking about winning the Tour de France. I am not even contemplating it. There are three big days to go and a hard time trial to come. I'll take each day and each climb as it comes and we will see what happens.

Going into the rest day, Thomas led Froome by 1 minute and 39 seconds, with Dumoulin a further 11 seconds behind. It was another day survived, but Thomas would be without the help of Gianni Moscon in the final week. He admitted:

> Every day in the *peloton* is stressful, so it's nice not to fight for a day." There were more boos as he collected the yellow jersey.
>
> It's not a nice situation because this is a highlight of my career. It's a massive honour and a privilege to be wearing the jersey and it's been an incredible race so far. There's obviously been a bit of negativity, which isn't nice, but you have to stay strong in your head and crack on. The way I see it, I would rather be in this jersey, having the race of my life and getting booed for whatever, than being dropped on the first climb and everyone cheering you.

Elsewhere, I sensed a change in the air. More and more people were now backing Thomas to keep his lead. In a straw poll of riders and team directors, the majority felt he could survive the last week. "I'm going all in," said Chris Boardman on ITV. "I think he's going to win it!" I didn't dare hope, and put some money on Froome and Dumoulin as an insurance policy.

23 July – Rest day

Geraint Thomas

THERE WERE QUESTIONS being asked in France by a frustrated public and the usual cynical voices. How could Thomas come from nowhere to win the Tour? After all, he had never finished higher than 15th, and five years earlier he had finished 140th. But I wasn't having that. He had ridden that Tour with a broken pelvis, after all! Anybody could pull out isolated race results as evidence for suspicion, but there is a deeper story, a consistent narrative to Geraint Thomas's career which shows natural progression. Lance Armstrong would later argue that Thomas's development into a Tour de France winner was far from unusual:

> His career trajectory has been pretty classic. He was a track rider, he was bigger and heavier, and he's got more and more experienced, obviously. But he's got lighter and leaner and much, much stronger and that culminates with what we saw over the last three weeks. Nobody can argue that he was not the best rider in the race.

Armstrong was right. A closer look at Thomas's development shows how he became the rider he is today.

Maindy Velodrome sits inconspicuously on the left-hand side of the A470 as you enter Cardiff from the north. Built in 1951, it used to be a major multi-sport stadium with track and field events and boxing matches taking place in front of a large grandstand. The cycle track was used for the 1958 Commonwealth Games, but there is little evidence now that this was once Cardiff's main athletics venue. The area was renovated in 1993 and a new swimming pool was built alongside the open air track. Two years after it opened, a nine-year-old Geraint Thomas went swimming at Maindy Pool. The pool's entrance looked out onto the track, and young Geraint saw children taking cycling lessons. The cycling coach, Debbie Wharton, lent him a bike, and the rest is history.

At first, Wharton noticed only his 'skinny legs'. But he showed a natural aptitude for cycling and his balance was good. He began to win races. Two years later he was joined at the Maindy Flyers Youth Cycling Club by a seven year old called Luke Rowe. Luke's father Courtney told Wales Online:

> Luke was good, but Geraint was just brilliant. Geraint was very rarely off the top step and always seemed to be coming home with the gold.

At Whitchurch High School, where Gareth Bale and Sam Warburton were also pupils, Thomas played other sports, but cycling gradually became his favourite. According to Debbie Wharton, there were early examples of the bravery that would define Thomas's career:

> He was always crashing his bike. He used to fall off a lot but he was also the quickest at getting back up.

Geraint hasn't forgotten his early coaches either – during the 2018 Tour, the yellow jersey-wearer took time to send a video message to Debbie Wharton's ill daughter.

In 1999, British Cycling was awarded significant long-term funding by the National Lottery and in 2003 an Academy was formed, based around Manchester Velodrome. Academy manager Rod Ellingworth recalls having his attention drawn to Thomas by one of the coaches at the national track championships. "Look at this kid. Look how aerodynamic he is. Look how small he makes himself across the front." Thomas had already won a race at the World Junior Championships in Los Angeles in 2004, aged 18. He told *Cycling News*:

> I guess I started to really believe in myself after Los Angeles. I started to see cycling as a career rather than a hobby. Up to then we just had fun riding bikes and we all went down to the Maindy track and it was just like a youth club really. From there I chose to go into the Academy rather than go to college.

He won the Junior Paris-Roubaix race that year, which was when I first became aware of his talent. Riding into the velodrome with Ian Stannard, his Great Britain teammate had turned the wrong way and left Geraint to cross the line first and celebrate alone. Even if they had sprinted together, "I still would have won", claimed Thomas. After that impressive result, Geraint Thomas was offered a place at the Academy and moved to Manchester, where he shared a house with fellow future Olympians Mark Cavendish and Ed Clancy.

In February 2005 came the crash in Australia that caused him to miss most of that season. After recovering, he spent time racing in Italy with the Great Britain Academy and experienced the animosity that would follow British riders across Europe throughout his career. Rod Ellingworth recalls that in one race, Geraint was dropped and riders and team cars mocked him as they passed. *'Inglese, Inglese!'* they shouted. "F***ing w***ers," he'd complained. "I'm not English – I'm Welsh!"

In 2007, Thomas signed with the Professional Continental cycling team, Barloworld. The South African sponsors had registered their team in Great Britain, and Thomas went to the Tour de France for the first time. There he supported sprinter Robbie Hunter alongside other teammates, including Kenyan rider Chris Froome. Photographs from this time show Thomas with a much rounder face than we're used to now. Of course, track riders don't need to climb and the extra weight is useful in the velodrome. He earned the nickname Penguin for a short while, due to his resemblance to one of the characters in the movie *Madagascar*. "He looks cuddly but every now and then you get a look from him which makes you realise he's anything but," said David Millar at the time.

Barloworld leader Robbie Hunter spoke of his time with the young Thomas in an interview with Gregor Brown:

> He was good, had a huge amount of talent and a motor, but he was about 10 kilograms heavier then. He was strong on the flats, helping me out in the sprints, but nowhere near to where he should have been climbing if you think he'd go on and win the Tour. I remember in one Tour stage, he was the first guy dropped and sucked it up until the last climb of the day, joining the *gruppetto* right at the base of the last climb. Most people would have called it a day after riding 99% on your own, but that showed a lot of character right there, especially as a 21 year old.

Thomas's manager at Barloworld, Claudio Corti, was impressed with the young rider's speed at the end of stages and saw him as a potential sprinter:

> There is no point in restricting him. We have to use races like the Tour to move him forward physically – you can see he has some fat to lose – but the key thing is that he can ride at 60 kilometres per hour.

Thomas was thinking along similar lines. He told *Cycling News* ahead of the Tour:

> I see myself as a lead-out man at the moment. I seem to be able to hold the top end for a long time and stay on the front from two kilometres out. Further down the line I would like to see what I could do in other races, like the one-day classics.

I spoke to Colin Lewis, who rode the Tour de France twice, for an article I wrote ahead of Geraint's debut Tour de France in 2007. "He won't finish," predicted Lewis. "He should be pulled out by his team before the mountains. If he even attempts to finish the race, it could destroy him." The youngest rider competing, Thomas did finish that race, despite suffering every day and coming in 140th out of the 141 who crossed the line in Paris.

In 2008, Thomas rode the Giro d'Italia, giving his manager Corti a sign of his Grand Tour potential late in the race. "Geraint finished the last day 12th in the time trial. That showed his motor and his ability to recover in a Grand Tour. He wanted to give it a go and he did well. There was something there. That was a sign." But Corti never saw Thomas as a potential winner. "He was a big *passista*, a strong motor, but no one was considering him for the climbs. It was only later when you had Bradley Wiggins transform and win the Tour that you thought something was possible. He was a big boy back then, how could he win the Tour?" he told *Cycling Weekly*. The Giro was undertaken as preparation for his main target that year – the Beijing Olympics. Thomas was part of the British team pursuit squad which broke the world record on its way to gold. It earned him an MBE, and importantly he was repaying the investment made by the GB Cycling Academy.

In this period, I was still disenchanted with professional cycling. The news from the Operación Puerto case, which revealed a sport riddled with drugs, had left me confused and disappointed. Like most cycling fans, I was ready for a new clean era, and there were noises coming from the *peloton* that they too had had enough. Geraint Thomas joined the growing chorus of protests about the doping culture. In 2008 his Barloworld teammate Moisés Dueñas was thrown off the Tour after failing a test for EPO. Thomas protested in his race blog:

> If someone is fraudulent in a business, wouldn't they be facing a prison term? I don't see how riders taking drugs to win races and lying to their teams is any different. Bang them up and throw away the key!

I liked what I was hearing and began to believe again.

At the end of a 2009 season disrupted by a broken pelvis suffered in the Tirreno-Adriatico race, Thomas left Barloworld and joined the newly formed Team Sky. In 2010, Thomas rode all the classics, but his only big win was the British National Road Race Championship. There were promising performances at the Critérium du Dauphiné and a spell in the young rider's jersey at the Tour de France. He was forced to pull out of the Delhi Commonwealth Games due to risk of infection after his splenectomy. He admitted:

> It's a massive disappointment. I only get to ride for Wales once every four years, but that's the decision I had to make.

2011 saw Thomas's first professional victory in the five-day Bayern-Rundfahrt race. He had a good Tour de France, wearing the white jersey (Best-placed Young Rider) for a week and finishing 31st overall. As an example of how unfair it is to compare Thomas's record in the Tour de France with his 2018 performance, we can look at this race. He had been well placed, wearing the white jersey, but stayed with his leader Bradley Wiggins after a crash, and lost over three minutes on a flat stage. He immediately dropped from 6th overall to 38th. The 2012 season was all about the London Olympics, with early road races ridden as preparation. He finished 2nd in both Giro Time Trials. Thomas took his second Olympic gold medal in the Team Pursuit event and a postbox in Castle Street, Cardiff was painted gold in recognition. A year later he was asked whether he would trade in his Olympic gold for the yellow jersey in the Tour de France:

> No. Winning that team pursuit Olympic gold medal was unbelievable. I just wouldn't do that.

The first sign that I saw as a fan that Geraint Thomas could become a GC rider was when he finished third at the Tour Down Under in 2013. With the Olympics over, Thomas was promoted to 'protected rider' status for Team Sky's classics season, which meant that he could rely on the full support of his team. I really enjoyed watching him race that year, as he returned from the track. But he couldn't stop crashing, going down at Roubaix, Flanders and Milan-San Remo. The worst crash of all that year came at the Tour, when he suffered a broken pelvis in the very first stage. In his book, *The World of Cycling According to G*, Thomas explained:

> It was without doubt the worst pain I have experienced on a bike. Each pedal stroke felt like being jabbed with a burning branch. Each tiny bump in the road felt like the branch was being rammed in a few twigs further. Trying to get out of the saddle to get over a slight rise was extraordinary. Trying to put some actual power down was like being sawn in half.

Despite the pain, Thomas rode another 2,000 miles and finished the race, again coming in 140th.

In 2014, he looked all set to take his biggest win on the road when he was contesting for the win at Paris-Nice. But again, he hit a tree on the penultimate stage and his race was effectively over. Top ten places at Flanders and Roubaix suggested that his future lay in the Classics. If he could stay upright, he could one day win a monument. At the time, I would have seen that as his greatest possible achievement, cementing his place among the leading Welsh sportsmen of all time. At the Tour that year, Thomas was a *domestique* to Chris Froome, who crashed early, and then to Richie Porte, who struggled. Thomas was left to ride for himself and finished a creditable 22nd. A week after the Tour finished, Thomas was in Glasgow, representing Wales in the Commonwealth Games.

In torrential rain and strong winds, he stormed clear of his rivals in a 12-lap race around the city centre. The race was gruelling, attritional, a test of character and bravery. Thomas was riding away to certain victory when disaster struck, and he punctured on the final lap. Obliged to take a wheel from the neutral service vehicle, the mechanic took what seemed like an eternity to make the change. With Jack Bauer and Scott Thwaites making ground, Thomas was forced to wait patiently. With admirable calm, he eventually remounted and set off again to take the gold medal. He crossed the line punching the air, pointing at the 'Wales' logo on his chest. I had never seen him so pumped at the end of a race. He said:

> It's up there alongside the Olympics and everything, to be honest. I've only got to race for Wales maybe once before in the whole of my senior career, so it's a great feeling.

In December, Thomas was voted BBC Wales Sports Personality of the Year.

2015 saw Thomas take overall victory on the Volta ao Algarve before another improved Classics season, threatening victory at Milan-San Remo before winning E3 Harelbeke, where his prize included his own weight in beer. He placed third in Gent-Wevelgem despite being blown off his bike by a freak gust of wind. Then came the sight of a very trim Geraint Thomas matching the best climbers in the mountains of the Tour of Switzerland, where he finished in second place by just five seconds. With his weight at 68 kg, he had lost 7 kg – approximately a stone – since his days as a track rider. It appeared that Geraint Thomas was moving into another gear, that he was on the verge of taking a major win.

The climbing form continued at the Tour de France, in service of Chris Froome. He shone in the Pyrenees, particularly impressing commentators when able to stay with the GC riders to the summit of Plateau de Beille. Taken out by a dramatic crash into a telegraph pole on the descent of the Col de Manse, Thomas was still able to hold 4th in GC and looked capable of a possible podium place. But on Stage 19, Thomas suffered what experienced riders call a *'jour sans'*, literally a 'day without' – a day during a long stage race where the rider wakes up feeling weak, without strength, without energy:

> I was just empty today. It was always going to happen, I guess. I was hoping it was going to happen on Monday but it happened today. As they say, sometimes you're the hammer, sometimes you're the nail. I was a cheap IKEA nail today. It was a tough start – when you've just got nothing in the legs, there's nothing you can do.

Thomas finished the Tour in 15th place, and this result was often referenced as evidence that he was unable to last the full three weeks at the head of General Classification. I admit that I was one of those who felt that his best chance of a win remained in the one-day races. But of course, he had spent the 2015 Tour working for Froome. He had expended energy that a leader would be able to preserve until those final few days. We wouldn't know whether Thomas could maintain a serious three-week challenge until he was able to ride as a leader. Former Tour rider Sean Yates was more confident, comparing him to Bradley Wiggins:

> Geraint Thomas is a phenomenon, he's a one of a kind almost. Obviously Bradley has won Olympic medals and won the Tour de

France, and Geraint looks like he can follow in his footsteps in
the long term.

Thomas himself was wondering whether he could compete for
the GC in different circumstances. "You can't help but think if
I'd ridden for myself this year, even without the support of the
team, would I have blown up when I did? I don't think I would
have, and maybe I could have hung on to a top five place," he
told *Cyclist* magazine. We were seeing the benefits of all the
weight loss since his days on the track.

At the start of 2016, Thomas spoke to *Ride Media* about the
fine margins of dieting.

> Even if I didn't watch my diet, I reckon I'd easily be down to
> 71 kg, just by riding my bike more and cutting back a bit but
> just doing more volume, and a [different] style of training – low
> intensity – you burn more fat anyway just because of that.
>
> I'd be a lot leaner anyway but then when you really knuckle
> down and you work with nutritionists and you really sort of plan
> what you're eating and things, it comes off even more. It's kind
> of infectious though. And that's when it can go bad because you
> think, 'Oh, I want to keep going... keep going!'
>
> Or, 'Oh, I'm 68 today and feel good so why can't I be 67 or 66?'
> And there is a point where it will all just fall away.

Thomas retained the Volta ao Algarve title in 2016 before
taking his best ever road win at Paris-Nice. Despite heavy
pressure from Alberto Contador on the final climb of the race,
Thomas was able to defend his lead by recovering time on the
descent and took the yellow jersey. He had been helped by Tony
Gallopin, one of Thomas's many friends in the *peloton*. It was
his first ever victory on the World tour. Thomas signed a new
contract with Team Sky, and as part of the new arrangement,

he would be able to enter the Grand Tours as a leader. Dave Brailsford confirmed as much when announcing the deal.

> He has gone from strength to strength, and winning Paris-Nice this year was another step up. I think it gave him real confidence and now he can set his sights on developing his performances in the Grand Tours. I still believe the best is yet to come from Geraint and we will enjoy supporting him to see just how far he can go.

Thomas repeated his previous year's 15th-place finish at the 2016 Tour de France, where he rode again as one of the world's best super-*domestiques* and helped Chris Froome to win his third Tour. But Geraint had been struggling that year with weight management, as he told *Cycling News*. He had misjudged the fine margins that he had spoken about at the start of the year.

> Going into the Tour I wasn't sure how I was going to ride. My weight had been up and down and it wasn't what I was used to. When I've gone to the Tour before I've been confident but this year it was totally different. I just pushed it too far with the weight loss, losing the last bit too quickly.

The news came that Thomas would share the Team Sky leadership at the 2017 Giro d'Italia with Mikel Landa. The announcement in January signalled a progression, a new era, and when Geraint won the Tour of the Alps ahead of Thibaut Pinot, his climbing ability was proven again. He was now ultralean, not carrying an ounce of unnecessary weight. But he had retained the power which had won him those races on the track and was able to use his extraordinary physical ability to win an Alpine stage race. He was evolving, but would he judge the weight loss well enough to take a podium place in the Grand Tours?

Sadly we wouldn't find out, as Thomas crashed out in both the Giro and the Tour de France, having worn the yellow jersey at the Tour after winning the prologue on the opening day. If these crashes had not happened, we might well have seen Thomas on the podium in one or both of these races. After starting with so much promise, 2017 had proved to be a season of frustration, as Geraint admitted after his crash in the Tour.

> I'll be able to go back on the bike really soon. Goals-wise, I don't know. I'll leave it a week, let the dust settle and decide what will motivate me until the end of the season. At the moment I just want to go down the pub.

2018 was the year when it all came right. All those crashes, mechanicals and misfortune were at last balanced by some good fortune on the other side of the karma scales. A combination of factors finally allowed Geraint Thomas to compete in a Grand Tour on his own terms, without the burden of team duties and without the interference of Lady Luck. At last we would see what a fit, focussed, prepared Geraint Thomas could do. It was time for that potential and all that promise to be fulfilled.

STAGE 16

Carcassonne to Bagnères-de-Luchon

THE CRUCIAL PYRENEES stages began with controversy, when Dave Brailsford suggested that spitting at riders was a "French cultural thing." Naturally, the Team Sky principal was upset about the way his riders had been treated, but did he really think those remarks would help the riders on the road? We would find out on the way to Luchon.

Bagnères-de-Luchon is a great base for the Tour when it reaches the Pyrenees. The old spa town is elegant and quirky, and a lot of fun when the Tour's in town, with lots of bars and restaurants. We were on our way home from one during the 2014 Tour when I spotted someone familiar. Standing on the pavement next to a large grey-haired tourist was Chris Boardman, the former Olympic Champion, Tour rider and now a presenter for ITV. The pair were protesting to an old lady who was determined to frame her photograph perfectly.

"Just get on with it! Take the bloody photo," shouted the tourist. "Come on! Please!" pleaded Boardman.

The lady was stubbornly ignoring her husband's protests, along with those of that man he wanted in her photograph.

"I want to get the hotel in the picture so that people can see where we're staying."

"Never mind that!" he shouted back. "Just get him and me in the photo."

Boardman was looking frustrated but he remained acquiescent as the woman barked instructions.

"Move a bit to the left. That's it. Now step forward."

By now the scene had attracted the attention of quite a large group of cycling fans who recognised the subject of her photograph. They too began heckling the lady.

"Take the bloody photo!" "Let him go back to his meal!" "Leave the guy alone!"

The embarrassed husband strode forward furiously to have a quiet word with his stubborn wife. As he implored her quietly to please take the photograph and be done with it, I saw my opportunity and darted in to stand alongside Chris Boardman while my wife quickly snapped a photo. "Thanks, Chris!" I blurted out, before hurrying away. He fumed under his breath and looked at his watch.

My children were still very young on that Tour and we adapted our plans accordingly. My wife and the two youngest boys entertained themselves in the town while my 14-year-old son Gruff and I rode out to the Port de Balès, which was the final climb in that day's race. Embarrassingly, Gruff dropped me early on the climb and refused to wait. I was feeling really bad and wanted to stop, but I knew that my firstborn child was somewhere on the long road ahead. I had seriously underestimated the Port de Balès and found it one of the toughest climbs I had ever ridden. In glaring sun, I was forced to take shelter more than once, and drink water from a stream.

I ploughed on up through the large crowds who were waiting along the route for the day's race. This lot weren't so supportive and some mocked my fat-bloke efforts. I was dismayed to reach the summit and see thousands of people at the top. It took me half an hour to find Gruff and he was beaming in the crowd. A tall Spanish cyclist had seen him riding the mountain and had begun chatting. On finding that the boy was riding alone, he'd accompanied him all the way up the climb, with fans cheering him on from the side. I felt that strange mixture of pride and shame that is felt by any cycling father when he gets dropped by his son.

We had planned to ride back down and join the rest of the family at the finish line in Luchon but the *gendarmes* were having none of it. They had closed the route and that was the end of it. What followed was like a slapstick silent movie routine. We would cycle down until we spotted another pale-blue police shirt, at which point we would dismount and stroll past, whistling innocently. It took ages to get down like that and we were pulled up and warned more than once. But nevertheless, we made it to join the rest of the family at a café before popping out to see the race arrive on our doorstep.

The next day would also be a compromise. Our 9 and 11 year olds were not keen on climbing a mountain so we strolled an hour up the route and found a perfect spot for freebie-snaffling. Every day, a long train of publicity vehicles travels ahead of the race. Known as the caravan, the convoy is 12 kilometres long and takes about 35 minutes to pass by. Over 600 people fill 160 floats and throw out 14 million gifts over the course of the Tour, ranging from keyrings and small sausages to team caps and shirts. It is difficult to explain the appeal of the caravan, but it's an extraordinary thing to witness. Beautiful girls and handsome lads dance in safety harnesses to blaring Europop, Vittel trucks spray giant water cannons over sweltering crowds, a giant plastic cyclist sits atop a big red lorry, while a fleet of 2CVs throw out floppy hats.

There are well-developed tactics used to gather the most souvenirs. Some families take upturned umbrellas to catch their booty. Sedate, smiling parents turn into rabid beasts when the caravan approaches, battling for every trinket thrown out from a truck. I was once pushed into a hedge by an 80-year-old grandmother as we grappled for a branded inflatable pillow. She shrugged when I complained – *"C'est Le Tour,"* she explained. In a recent poll, 47% of people at the roadside claimed that they were there for the caravan. Our small children agreed – that was definitely the highlight of their day.

We took our spot on the roadside out of Luchon with a cliff wall behind us. The boys spread out and gave angelic smiles to the caravan as it passed. Any loot that they missed hit the back wall and was collected later. It was our best ever tally – we left with bags full of hats, bags, T-shirts, caps and crucially plenty of madeleine cakes and Haribo sweets. We were joined on the road by some more of Team Sky's strange supporters. This pair had bought nine inflatable aliens and attached masks of each member of the team. The Sky riders had all signed their aliens – I can only imagine what they made of their odd groupies.

We watched the *peloton* pass by and headed back to a Luchon bar to watch the rest of the race. I love watching cycling in a bar or a café in the company of the French. They know their cycling and it's great to see them react instinctively, like we would if we were watching a football or rugby match. When Rafał Majka rode away effortlessly past Visconti to win the stage that year, he winked at the camera and the bar exploded with laughter. An old man caught my eye and injected an imaginary needle into his arm. He had seen these sorts of rides before.

The 2018 stage from Carcassonne to Bagnères-de-Luchon was a day for descending carefully. The stage included the Col de Portet d'Aspet, notorious as the place where Olympic Champion Fabio Casartelli crashed and died in 1995. Then came the Col de Menté, the scene of a famous stage involving Eddy Merckx and Luis Ocaña in 1971. Both riders crashed, Ocaña was injured and Merckx refused to wear the yellow jersey out of respect.

In 2018 it was Philippe Gilbert causing concern, when he flew over a low wall on the Col de Portet d'Aspet and dropped heavily onto a pile of stones. On a day full of drama, protesting French farmers interrupted the race near Toulouse. This, again, is not too uncommon and the *gendarmes* were ready, dispersing them with pepper spray. Unfortunately, the wind carried the spray into the *peloton*, affecting many riders –

114

including Chris Froome and Geraint Thomas, who were forced to stop and wipe their weeping eyes. Luke Rowe was also affected and none were too impressed, as Rowe's tweet shows:

Popped my pepper spray cherry today, not a cool experience.

Yet another of Thomas's potential challengers suffered a crash. Adam Yates was looking set to win the stage when he went down on the final descent of the day, allowing Julian Alaphilippe to take his second stage. I like Alaphilippe. He's a real *puncheur*, specialising in rolling terrain with short, steep climbs. Always smiling, he has a great relationship with his French fans and revels in the attention he receives. I think about Julian Alaphilippe almost every night. I'm not sure whether I should admit to this, but he helps me sleep. If my mind is too alert and I'm finding it difficult to doze off, I play a game. I try to name a cyclist whose surname begins with each letter of the alphabet, and I always start with Alaphilippe. It works well. I've never yet got past Vincenzo Nibali, as I'm always snoozing by the time I reach the letter 'O'.

Julian Alaphilippe burst onto the scene in 2015 with a couple of second places at the Ardennes Classics, three famous one-day races held in April in the Ardennes area of Belgium and the Dutch Limburg region. The three races – Amstel Gold Race, La Flèche Wallonne and Liège-Bastogne-Liège – are not my favourites. Although I enjoy watching, for me they don't have the same drama and chaotic unpredictability as Paris-Roubaix or the Tour of Flanders.

Geraint Thomas's race calendar does not usually include the Ardennes Classics, but in 2018, with his season focussed on the Tour de France, he rode Liège-Bastogne-Liège for the first time. Known as *La Doyenne*, or The Old Lady, Liège-Bastogne-Liège is one of the oldest and most prestigious races in professional cycling. The 260 km course is filled with short climbs, and Thomas would use it to build up strength ahead of his main objective. He finished 56th, rolling in over 3 minutes behind Bob Jungels. But this race was not his target in 2018.

Thomas's target – his whole focus this year – was the Tour de France, and he would be entering the final week of that race in the yellow jersey after his team controlled Stage 16 to maintain his lead. At 32, and with every daily obstacle and barrier so far overcome, he would never get a better chance. But he'd been in a good position before entering the final week, and never managed to finish better than 15th. Of course, 2018 was different. The road had decided that he was now the leader of the best team in world cycling, and he just had to stay calm, keep his nerve, and navigate some of the most formidable mountains in Europe. The High Pyrenees were looming.

"It wasn't the day to go for an all-out attack," said Dumoulin, who was now surely the only rider that could threaten Thomas and Froome. "I need to keep my powder dry." ITV's Chris Boardman felt that the next stage would decide the Tour:

> The big question is about Geraint Thomas – will he have that bad day? Because if he's going to have one, it's going to be tomorrow… If he gets through tomorrow with the same lead, then you'd think that the team would say, 'Right, we'd better get behind him'.

STAGE 17

Bagnères-de-Luchon to Saint-Lary-Soulan

THE TOUR WAS now deep in the heart of the Pyrenees, an area I rode for the first time in 2012. I had known Tommie Collins for a long time, as we both followed the Welsh national football team. But I hadn't realised that Tommie was a keen cyclist, and when I mentioned visiting the Tour that year, I was surprised that he was so enthusiastic about making the trip. "We can ride the Tourmalet," he suggested. The Tourmalet? Gulp. I was doing well in recovery from illness and had completed a couple of easy sportives but I didn't think I was ready for a climb like that. But Tommie is nothing if not persuasive, and I found myself unpacking my bike outside a hotel in Argelès-Gazost a few days before the Tour arrived.

We rode up to Luz Ardiden as a warm-up. That 'warm-up' was the toughest climb of my life at that point. I wasn't ready for the average 7% gradient over 15 km. It was brutal, and it hurt a lot. My legs were aching badly and my arse was sore for the whole hour and a half that it took me to climb the road where Lance Armstrong had been derailed by a shopping bag. I averaged about 5 mph while Tommie rode ahead. Still, I got there eventually, and I was reasonably confident that the Tourmalet could be conquered the next day.

We rose early and spun the 20 km to the foot of the famous climb in the village of Luz-Saint-Sauveur. The whole area was buzzing with fans and cyclists who had come to watch the Tour pass through the following day. It was a sunny morning and I was terrified of burning my ginger skin on the climb. The air was cool in the shadows and I knew that weather could change at the summit, wary after my experience on the Galibier. With a cold descent in mind, I wore a long-sleeved jersey as I carefully began to climb the lower slopes to the village of Barèges. I was passed regularly by one fit cyclist after another. One particularly tanned, oily young man slowed beside me and started gesticulating wildly. After a while, I realised he was suggesting strongly that I remove my top. "You're crazy, you will boil," he advised. I winked nonchalantly as if I was holding a secret.

The climb took about three hours, and I was suffering for every second of that time. But I refused to stop. To me, the achievement wouldn't count if I had climbed off the bike, even for a few minutes. The challenge was to complete it in the saddle without taking a rest. On and on it went. First discomfort, then pain, and for the last hour, agony. It took all my willpower to stay on that bike and keep those pedals moving, metre by metre, turn by turn. Never mind pedalling squares, I was pedalling octagons. I was overheating too, as my friend had warned – like a boil-in-the bag cod. I saw him on his way back down the mountain and he waved, laughing as he went.

The Tourmalet is a climb which you constantly believe must end around the next corner. On and on it goes, until you reach a plateau where a hundred motorhomes are parked up for the race. This must be the top, you surmise, until a glance up the mountain reveals more hairpins climbing impossibly into the clouds. Nonetheless, I carried on. I had to. And finally, somehow, I found myself in the company of hundreds of other riders who were blocking the 2,000 metre summit road beneath the memorial to Jacques Goddet. Tommie was among them and he looked disappointingly fresh. "I enjoyed that," he laughed, in Welsh.

One of the most memorable things about that day was the descent of the Tourmalet. After leaving the strong smell of burning clutches at the summit, and sounds of screeching brakes on the hairpin descent, I let the bike ease into the long straight, fast open road. Now, I'm a big man and it doesn't take much for me to build up a head of steam. At first I was thrilled to be able to career down that long wide slope, passing more timid, lighter cyclists who had flown by me so easily on the way up. Faster and faster I went.

I started to go really fast. I found myself going faster than I had ever gone in my life. I glanced down at the computer and saw that I had passed 80 kph and was still gaining speed. I was in unknown territory, and I knew that a slight wobble, a pothole, or maybe just a small stone could bring me down. Finally, and more crucially, I just didn't trust those skinny wheels on that featherweight tube of carbon to carry me down safely. I felt like I was in a rocket that was entering space for the first time, and I panicked. I slowed down and made sure that I got to the bottom in one piece.

That day on the Tourmalet still ranks as one of my toughest days on the bike, beaten only by the 2012 Wild Wales Challenge, which climbed the brutal Bwlch y Groes, and the 2015 Conwy Gran Fondo. It is the single toughest ascent I've ever undertaken, just ahead of the Port de Balès, another Pyrenean giant. The Tourmalet would come later in the 2018 Tour, but the Stage 17 route did take in the Col de Peyresourde, which is a beautiful bucolic ride out of Bagnères-de-Luchon.

The Col de Peyresourde was first included in the 1910 Tour de France, on a stage which was so tough it was known as the 'Circle of Death'. In 1937, French rider Roger Lapébie was warming up to climb the Peyresourde at the start of that day's stage when his bike fell apart. He had been sabotaged by rivals. I've always loved learning about the history of cycling, with so much controversy, drama and skulduggery of all forms. Recent races have seen a crackdown on riders who hold on to team cars for a lengthy period. It's common for riders to request a drink and clasp the bottle for a few seconds when it is proffered from the car by the outstretched hand of the *Directeur Sportif*. The practice, known as 'taking a sticky bottle', is tolerated unless a rider takes obvious liberties.

By Stage 17 in 2018, Arnaud Démare was one of only a few sprinters left in the Tour after a whole batch, including André Greipel, had been eliminated by the time-cut rule in the second week. Rules state that each rider must finish within a certain percentage of the winner's time every day. Démare was dropped early on the day's first climb and looked destined to miss the cut-off, which would have seen him ejected from the Tour. He finished second last on the stage, 29 minutes behind Quintana, but within the cut-off time. A watching André Greipel was sceptical, as this tweet shows:

> Maybe someone should tell FDJ and Arnaud Démare that there is GPS tracking in Le Tour. *Chapeau* to lose just 9 min on a 17 km climb on Quintana. #notforthefirsttime

With that hashtag, Greipel was referring to Démare's 2016 victory at Milan-San Remo, which had been followed by accusations that he had held onto a team car to recover after crashing at the foot of the key climb. Greipel was implying that Démare had received help illegally. Démaré was furious and responded with a tweet of his own:

> Glad to know you don't respect me as much as I respect you. I thought you were smarter. There are jury members everywhere at all times. I'm sending you my files. Given that you are an expert, let's see what you think about it.

Greipel would apologise publicly for the accusations, but the Frenchman was unimpressed. Ahead of Stage 18, Démare responded:

> Unfortunately, his apology doesn't do a whole lot because the damage is done. It's opened a door for people to doubt. Now people will think what they want. But there are more commissaires this year, there is the video commissaire this year as well, which means they are omnipresent.

Stage 17 began with a gimmicky grid start, similar to Formula

1 motor races. As expected, the grid had no effect as riders soon organised themselves as usual. At just 65 km long and including three major climbs, it was expected to be an explosive day that would test Thomas. I watched it nervously in the television room of a campsite in the Loire, having agreed with my friend Scott that we would head down to the Pyrenees if Geraint was still in contention at the end of the day.

The route started immediately with a climb up the Peyresourde. This was then followed by the Col de Val Louron-Azet and finally, the toughest climb of the day, the Col de Portet. Approximately 38 km of the total 65 km would be climbs, with almost no flat roads included on the stage. That final climb on the Col de Portet was where Nairo Quintana attacked. At four minutes behind, Quintana was no danger to Thomas or Froome, and he rode away with Dan Martin for a fantastic win. But the real story of the day was taking place further down the hill, where Chris Froome was making a concerted effort to put himself back in the race for yellow.

Roglič went first, and Froome went with him. This could be the decisive move, and Geraint must have been anxious. But he was patient and sat on the wheel of Dumoulin. This was a good move, as the Dutchman was forced to bring back the attacking pair. Sky riders Egan Bernal and Wout Poels were still there in support of their leaders.

Roglič attacked again, and took Thomas and Dumoulin with him. But where was Froome? He seemed to be in trouble and the loyal Egan Bernal stayed to help drag him back to the group. But Dumoulin smelt blood and went again with 2 km left. This was a breathless cat and mouse chase now, with Roglič going once more before Thomas darted out at the finish to gain another 5 seconds on the pair. The Welshman looked strong and confident and, dramatically, he had finished 48 seconds ahead of Froome, who could not respond in the final. The result meant that Thomas now led the Tour by 1 minute 59 seconds from Dumoulin, with Froome 2 minutes 31 seconds back. Thomas was then asked about the situation regarding team leadership, which was now surely in his hands.

> We've just been open and honest with each other from the start. Maybe it's hard to believe sometimes after the situation with him and Brad. But we genuinely are good mates, and we're honest and open and I think that is the main reason for success for the team.

Thomas went on to speak about Froome's tactics. "He wanted to try to do something so he went early with Roglič," he said. "I just assumed he was going to be good. He wasn't feeling too great towards the top." For his part, Froome seemed to have conceded leadership of the team. "We've just got to try and look after him now, these next few days," he muttered, evidently disappointed with the day's outcome. I was warily unconvinced. I still wasn't sure whether this was a bluff. I had seen Froome recover from lost positions before and I wouldn't be able to relax until the end of the time trial in Espelette. Anything might happen before then. There had even been drama towards the end of the stage, when Geraint Thomas was grabbed by a burly spectator wearing an AG2R shirt who leaned across the barrier.

Obviously it's not good and I won't be riding quite so close to the barriers. I could have quite easily fallen and lost a bit of time. I was going quite fast past him but it certainly moved me off my line. It was a bit of a shock, but luckily I was OK. But obviously it wasn't nice. We come here to race our bikes and that's all we want to do. The whole *peloton* just wants to do that safely. It's a bit too much.

Three seconds after Thomas had crossed the line, my phone rang. It was Scott. "Are you watching? We've got to go, haven't we?"

STAGE 18

Trie-sur-Baïse to Pau

I LEFT BRISSAC-QUINCÉ with my son Gruff at 7 a.m. The Peugeot hire car was small, cramped, but satisfyingly French. We wound our way down through the grids of minor roads onto the huge 100-mile stretches of toll roads where we paid a fortune in charges. I usually enjoy the French *péage* when I'm driving the motorhome, as my wife sits on the left. As we approach, I make sure to keep a bit of distance between the vehicle and the ticket machine. She is then left completely defenceless when I slap her arse as she stretches out and leans over to collect the ticket. She knows it's coming, but there is absolutely nothing she can do about it.

The *péage* is not as much fun when I'm driving a French car. It's me that has to do all the work at the ticket machine and the pressure builds as I join the end of the queue. What if the machine breaks? What if it doesn't recognise my card? What if I can't find my ticket? The French toll machine is a terrifying thing, and I have nightmares about blocking hundreds of angry French motorists as I fumble for change.

We hit Bordeaux in good time, but that's when the problems

started. Roadworks and heavy traffic saw the *'Bouchons'* sign flashing regularly to warn of jams ahead. And these were proper jams, which saw us take two hours to get across town to the airport where we were collecting Scott. I was rapidly losing my sense of humour as I realised we might not even catch the finish in Pau. But then, out of nowhere, we found ourselves right outside the Stade de Bordeaux where I had seen Wales beat Slovakia in the 2016 Euros. They even still had the giant Euro 2016 sign on the concourse.

I was still grinning and reminiscing with Gruff when we drove in to pick up Scott from Bordeaux-Mérignac Airport. Now, Scott is a huge man. He is 6' 5" tall, and weighs in at 19 stone. With a bald pate and a large white beard, he has been fairly compared (in looks, at least) to South African white supremacist Eugène Terre'Blanche. Scott took his place in the front seat of the tiny Peugeot, with his bare knees splayed wide, forcing me to push them away every time I wanted to change gear. It wouldn't be the last time that intimacy was forced upon us on that trip.

Nine hours after leaving Brissac, we approached Pau from the west. It was then I realised I had made a basic Tour de France error – booking a hotel on the wrong side of town. Somehow, I was going to have to cross the race route. I dropped Scott and Gruff off in the centre of town and then drove blindly around barriered roads. Miraculously, I somehow found myself in front of the Ibis Budget, our home for the night. As I crossed the car park, I heard Welsh voices. I turned round to see Rhodri Gomer from S4C's *Seiclo* programme, sitting at the wheel of an accredited press car and about to lanyard-flash his way to the finish line. I quickly counted S4C bodies and available car seats to crushingly realise that my only way to the line would be to walk along the race route.

It was scorching hot. I could feel my skin frying as I passed the 2 km banner. I had missed the caravan and parents and children were already streaming away from the route. Another kilometre and more frying. I remembered from my last visit to a Pau stage that bars were infrequent on the route, but this was surely the most alcohol-free stretch of road in France. Eventually, I saw a sign for Hoegaarden and dived into the most refreshing air-conditioned bar that you could wish for. And the race was on the telly. Scott and Gruff joined me, and I was even tempted to sit there and just nip out to see the *peloton* pass. I knew from experience that a sprint finish can be a bit dull, and places near the line were reserved for VIPs, so I wasn't desperate to get closer. But Geraint was in yellow and would be collecting his jersey. It would be a crying shame to drive all that way and not be there to see him at the presentation. After all, this might be his last day in the famous jersey. On we went, squeezing past the thicker crowds that blocked the narrow pavements with the line in sight. We grabbed a place at the side of the road and soon the race arrived.

Whoosh! The awesome sound and power of a fast-moving *peloton* can be felt as it gears up for a sprint. The riders are focussed, the game is on, and a huge draught of wind catches spectators by surprise as a single block of 100 riders travel en masse at speeds approaching 50 mph. But they were gone in an instant, with a few stragglers following in behind, their work completed earlier on in the day. And we were gone too

127

– weaving our way purposefully to the presentation area beyond the finish line.

There were quite a few Welsh people around and we waved our flags at the back of the crowd which had already gathered in front of the stage. It's never great access at the presentations with such a large area reserved for press and hangers-on, and Geraint was some distance away. We struggled, too, on the flag front. I had left my big flag in Wales and was lucky to borrow a small one that had been produced by BBC Wales for the 2005 rugby Grand Slam. I still see loads of those flags about, so that was a good piece of marketing by the Beeb. The locals peered at the writing – why did my flag say 'BBC Cymru' on it? What did that mean? I didn't try to explain. Scott was similarly flagless. The only thing he carried was a 6ft beach towel printed on one side with the red dragon.

This was my first experience of the French public's attitude towards Geraint on this tour, and his reception was definitely mixed as he collected the yellow jersey in Pau. Cheers sound a lot like boos when they are mixed together, so it was hard to tell what the split was. But there definitely were boos, which annoyed me. One of the things that made me so proud about Geraint was his popularity. He was a fantastic ambassador for Wales and here he was being booed for his connection to Team Sky. Ah well – sod them. I cheered loudly, as did the small group of Welsh people in front of me.

After the presentations finished and the crowds dispersed, I saw Rhodri Gomer at the barriers. "Yeah, I've just finished interviewing Geraint – he's as calm as he usually is, you know?" I didn't know, because I've never met him. And to be honest, I like it that way. I became too involved in football and worked for a while at Cardiff City – the club I'd supported all my life. But getting to know the players and experiencing the behind-the-scenes goings on spoiled it for me. It was much more fun when players were my heroes, and a football match felt special. I don't want to lose the magical appeal of the Tour and I'm happy to keep my distance.

I did an interview for S4C and was cheerfully expressing my delight at being there when Peter Sagan walked by. I was genuinely star-struck and had to stop the interview. I pointed with my jaw on the floor... "That's... that's... Peter Sagan..." There was the greatest cyclist in the world, standing a few feet away from me. Rhodri looked a bit bemused at my reaction. I was a 50-year-old grown man behaving like a teenage girl, while he rubs shoulders with riders like Sagan every day. But I make no apologies for that. I'm an unashamed fan.

And then a few minutes after my interview with Rhodri, I got what I was hoping for when Geraint Thomas himself stepped onto the road. He was being shepherded around by half a dozen officials, presumably going to another press call, or maybe a drugs test. I instinctively called out to him from the other side of the street. I even put on a thicker-than-usual Welsh accent so that he would hear it above the crowd.

"GERAINT! WELL DONE, MATE! NICE ONE!"

He looked across in my direction as Scott took an embarrassed step backwards.

"WE'RE PROUD OF YOU, GERAINT!"

He raised an eyebrow and nodded back, tentatively waving across. I noticed how skinny he was. His legs were like matchsticks. His thighs didn't meet and he moved with the certainty of a newborn foal. Cyclists aren't great at walking.

He looked as lean as he could be – there was not an ounce of fat on his tendons and muscles. His eyes were sunk into the back of his head and he gazed blankly. This was a man who was at his physical limit and evidently exhausted by his efforts. How on earth could he look like this, get up the next day and do it all again?

"THANK YOU, GERAINT! THANK YOU!"

He nodded again and raised a hand in recognition once more. I could sense Scott wishing that I would let it go. But I couldn't. This is why I was here – to let him know the whole country was behind him.

"I'VE BEEN WAITING 20 YEARS FOR THIS, GERAINT!"

What? Where did that come from? Why did I shout that? It wasn't true. I hadn't been waiting for it, as I had never imagined it was possible. And why 20 years? That would have taken me back to 1998, which is the date of my wedding and the year I watched Pantani win on the Galibier. But it definitely wasn't a year where I had started waiting for Geraint Thomas to win the Tour de France.

Scott looked at me with a smirk. "He's terrified of you. You know that, don't you? He's just asked that security guy to keep you away from him." I told Scott to bugger off, but he persevered. "He's thinking, 'Who's that fat little ginger bloke with the big gob, shouting gibberish across the road? Why is he waving a towel at me?' He thinks you're mad."

I knew he was right. But as Geraint Thomas was whisked away, I was pleased that I'd had the chance to let him know what this meant to us. Scott was still ribbing me as we supped cool beer in a nearby bar. By 9 p.m. I was telling anybody who would listen how Geraint and I had discussed the race for a while after the stage finish. By 11 p.m. I had trouble telling anybody anything, but I do remember meeting legendary Irish rider Sean Kelly on the street. I shook his hand and he waited for me to say something. "I'm sorry," I mumbled. "I haven't thought of anything to say – I just wanted to meet you." He looked at me just like Geraint at looked at me, with a heady mixture of bewilderment and fear.

STAGE 19

Lourdes to Laruns

THE TOUR DE France can be enjoyed in many ways. The key to a successful day at the side of the road lies in a simple algorithm which should help inform your decisions. I'll give it a go.

$$\text{enjoyment} = \frac{\text{preferred location}}{\text{inconvenience}}$$

I'll explain.

Before you plan your trip to the Tour, you need to consider how much effort and inconvenience you are prepared to endure in order to watch the race from your ideal position. For example, a position at the summit of a mountain finish will normally mean an overnight stay and a late departure, while you can pop over to a nondescript place on the day's route and be gone in half an hour. It's all about balance.

I've watched the Tour in a number of ways, from sleeping on the mountain to watching a stage roll out quietly just yards from my campsite gate. Each option has its merits. Ask yourself what you want to achieve: is this a day where you need to watch at the crucial point of the race action, or would you prefer to see the *peloton* weave past from the patio of a convenient bistro? And of course there are infinite options in between. We had one of those pay-off decisions to make on Stage 19 in 2018.

We knew that Geraint Thomas's fate would be influenced greatly by this final mountain stage from Lourdes to Laruns. We ran through the options and the implications of each choice. Our first instinct was to see the riders start at Lourdes. It can be fun to experience the ceremonies of a start town and it gives you a great opportunity to get up close to the riders. You get to witness the whole chaotic buzz of race preparation, from the playing of the local brass band to the mechanics who can be seen fine-tuning the bikes at the side of the road. Riders are relaxed and usually happy to chat and pose for photos. After they'd rolled off in Lourdes, we could get in the car and make our way to a place at the end of the route.

The finish town was out of the question today. From the map, Laruns appeared to offer only one main road in and out. Access and – more crucially – departure would be a nightmare, with inevitable long delays. The race would cross the legendary Tourmalet mountain, which would normally be the main attraction, but today it was an early climb of the day, and I knew that it would be a low-key point, with riders still sizing each other up.

I could see from the map that there was a side road that joined the course at the summit of the Col du Soulor, some 9 km short of the key point of the stage – the summit of the Col d'Aubisque. I had ridden these cols with Tommie Collins and I believed that we would know the outcome of the stage by the summit of the Soulor, which descends a little before climbing again to the Aubisque. That access road settled the deal. Even if we left at dawn, we could be waiting until midnight to get down off the Aubisque. The Soulor allowed us to witness a key part of the route and still get off the mountain in reasonable time. As we met for breakfast in the glamorous East Pau Ibis Budget Hotel, I made a late decision. I knew that the route to the Col du Soulor via the village of Arbéost would close once it became too busy. I made the call to forgo the start at Lourdes and drive straight for the hills. It was the right call.

I love the feeling of excitement and adventure as I head to a mountain stage – especially in the Pyrenees, which seem a little wilder, a little more untamed than the clean, Germanic, pine-covered Alps. We arrived at the foot of the mountain at about 10 a.m. and drove up the pass for 30 minutes, across ancient bridges over tumbling mountain streams. The narrow road turned and twisted through hamlets and villages as we passed group after group of amateur cyclists, all climbing to the summit. One of the differences between the Pyrenees and the Alps are the kilometre markers on the road indicating the distance to the summit, along with the average gradient of the next kilometre. This can be a welcome guide or a heart-sinking warning to the cyclist. But as I was driving up that morning, each kilometre of progress meant one less to walk to the summit of the Col du Soulor. Scott was beaming by now, as the glory of the mountains became evident. A long climb like this, even in a car, surpasses any similar drive you could experience in the UK. Distant cow bells rang across the rolling meadows as he climbed out to walk the last few metres to the top while we looked for somewhere to park.

It was absolute chaos up there. Cars, vans and motorhomes claimed every available space that was accessible from the road. Tents were pitched randomly on the hillside and experienced French spectators had laid out their picnic tables across empty parking spaces. Some had even gone so far as to stretch barrier tape from their vehicles to claim their area. The lack of organisation is surprising, but also refreshing in these days of rules and regulations. It was every man for himself up there, as blocked cars turned around to make their way back down the road. I inched my way down too, with regular logjams stopping my progress. Drivers were getting less choosy now and abandoning their cars in spaces that had been considered impossible an hour earlier. I pulled across to the side of the road about 2 km from the top, behind a London couple who were touring in a small converted builder's van.

I breathed in the clean mountain air and relieved myself in a grassy dip surrounded by dramatic snow-peaked summits. Cows stared at me as I mounted a Welsh flag on an extendable fishing rod. There was just enough room to add the blue and gold EU banner to show that I wasn't one of that Brexit lot. As we walked up to join Scott, we passed a *gendarme* who was in the process of closing the road. It had been a great decision to skip the start in Lourdes.

One of the reasons I had chosen the Soulor is that the facilities are good at the summit, and we were going to be

135

there for at least six hours. Amazingly, Scott had blagged a table outside one of the two cafés and we sat there most of the day, watching thousands of fans from all over the world pass us by. Some were in cycling kit or football shirts, others in national costume or fancy dress. Colourful flags from 50 nations and regions fluttered above the crowds. There were hot dog stalls, merchandise sellers, fire engines, police vans, and local producers selling cheese, bread and pâté. People who tell me that watching cycling lasts 30 seconds have no idea. It's about this – all of it.

The vista from the summit was extraordinary. Mist had risen in the valley and it would clear intermittently to reveal dramatic snow-peaked mountains which dominated the skyline. The light is different up there too – cleaner and sharper, the refined air today polluted only by the fumes of vehicles. In the distance, the roofs of hundreds of motorhomes glistened from the impromptu car park created lower down the race route. Those people had picked their spot a day or two earlier and would not leave until tomorrow. They had chosen the cycling fan's equivalent of a city break and one day I will watch a stage like that. But not today.

On one uneven ridge above the road, I spotted a van covered with a Welsh flag. The occupant was Arwyn Thomas from Caernarfon, who had travelled alone to every stage since the second day of the Tour. He'd had to miss yesterday's finish in Pau to find that rare patch of ground. We were kept entertained by a group of 'look at us!' teenagers who performed histrionics in fancy dress – among them a pantomime cow, a Super Mario and a Catholic priest who walked around blessing the crowd.

After a while the caravan approached. I let Scott and Gruff fight for the freebies, but they had little success. Their positioning was wrong, the caravan was too fast, and a 6' 5" beardy bald man with arms outstretched will always struggle for freebies. They returned with a paltry collection of leaflets, keyrings, and a couple of shopping bags-for-life. But Scott had managed to stretch out his giant frame and catch a Direct Énergie shirt intended for the blue-eyed six year old who was now weeping behind him.

The mist had deterred the camera helicopters so we had less warning than usual of the approach of the first riders. We knew that Sky had pulled back the early break, but we hadn't managed to get an update for the past 30 minutes. The anticipation of the riders' approach had been building for over six hours. Some people had been waiting on the mountain for days for the moment which was now imminent. We'd been part of a worldwide audience watching these athletes on television and very soon they would be live in front of our noses, competing closer to the fans than in any other sport.

For some people, the need to be part of the event they've seen on TV is more important than seeing the action. They are desperate to share the screen and make sure their actions make them visible. I could tell the shaven-headed Spanish lad to my right was one of those. We saw the first riders coming round the bend below. There was a small group, but who was in it? Suddenly, the Basque rider Mikel Landa appeared, deep eyes ahead, wide mouth open as he gave everything in his efforts to put the others in trouble. The Spanish lad sprinted alongside his hero, filling the safe space I had left between myself and the riders. I'd have hit him if I hadn't been afraid that he might topple into the road.

Landa was followed by a Bora-Hansgrohe rider and then the French went crazy for Romain Bardet. A minute later came the yellow jersey.

"GO ON, GERAINT! COME ON, MY SON! DIG IN!"

As Thomas passed – a picture of composed, single-minded focus, the Spaniard hurled insults. His thumb turned down, he shouted abuse in the face of our man. I squared up to him and let him have it. He looked nonplussed. He didn't really mean it – like a football fan who boos a ref, he was just playing his part in the pantomime. I let it go and watched Chris Froome struggle to catch the yellow jersey group. That was the best sight I'd seen all day. In my mind, Froome was still the biggest danger to Geraint, but I knew in that moment that he was definitely finished. Thomas had looked relatively comfortable and as long as he stayed upright, I now believed – for the first time – that he could win.

We watched and cheered on all the other riders in approval of their immense effort and just in simple love for the Tour de France. You often see and hear the words '*Vive Le Tour*', but the phrase comes to life on the roadside where spectators cheer the race itself, applaud all the riders and celebrate this awesome event. But amidst the drama, the euphoria, the excitement, cold logistics entered my head. The main race was gone and we were now cheering on individuals. Julian Alaphilippe high-fived the fancy-dress priest and others smiled and waved as they approached the end of the last real climb in the long, tough, three-week race. Relief started to spread on their faces, and their visible struggles were relatable to anyone who has churned their way up a steep hill. This is the part of the race you never see on the screen.

But we had a decision to make. Every minute longer we spent on that summit could cost an extra ten minutes to get off it. We hadn't seen Luke Rowe yet, but we had a three-hour drive to Biarritz ahead of us and it had already been a long day in the sun. If we left now, we could guarantee dinner and cold beer tonight. If we waited for Luke, it could mean a baguette from a garage and vending machine coffee. We left quickly, following the race on Scott's phone while slowly descending in a long stream of crawling cars.

Roglič took the stage, but Geraint Thomas finished safely, even gaining 6 more bonus seconds on Dumoulin. The day could hardly have gone better. He was now 2:05 ahead of Dumoulin and 2:24 in front of Roglič, with Chris Froome back in fourth at 2:37.

Of the effort to defend yellow on the last climbs, Thomas said:

> I had a good poker face for sure. I knew all I had to do was follow Tom Dumoulin. I knew he'd be chasing Roglič as well. Roglič was strong, man. He was going today, but it was all under control.

There was just one day left now – and if everything played out as expected, Geraint Thomas would win the Tour. We all knew it; we just couldn't bring ourselves to believe it.

Individual Time Trial – Saint-Pée-sur-Nivelle to Espelette

"COME TO BIARRITZ," implored Scott. "I've got a room booked." It seemed a better option than trawling the web to find somewhere near the Time Trial course. Biarritz centre had been booked up for weeks due to a Basque festival which saw thousands of people in white clothes and red scarves promenading around the city. And Scott had indeed booked a room. What I didn't know was that Scott had requested a double bed. "It's alright, I'll change it when we get there," he promised. He wasn't able to change it.

I've slept with Scott before. We'd shared a bed at a hotel next to Norwich City Football Club after an away game five years earlier. He's a big man and I'm a big man. It isn't easy to lie down on a double bed without our shoulders touching, but I was determined to try and avoid any contact at all. We agreed that Scott would sleep under the blanket while I would sleep on top. I lay wide awake most of the night, perched precariously as close to the side as possible, with my arm dangling over the edge. I eventually drifted off after playing the alphabet game. I still couldn't think of a current rider beginning with 'O'.

It was his breath on my back that awoke me at dawn. I jumped out of bed immediately, showered and crept downstairs to breakfast, where I found a coachload of American tourists leaving to find a good spot on the course. I sat at breakfast for three hours while my bed partner snored upstairs. The receptionist assumed that we'd had a lovers' tiff.

I hadn't been to a time trial for years. They leave me cold, to be honest, so the plan was to make sure we were there at the end with a good spot in front of the presentation if Geraint won the Tour (and yes, it was still an 'if', even though Dumoulin had effectively conceded). Gruff had spent the night with his mate Celyn, who was staying with relatives nearby. Celyn's father Rich joined us and he shared our Celtic gloom. "Prepare for the worst, hope for the best," he advised, with typical Welsh pessimism.

I love the Tour de France but I didn't enjoy that day much. It was the first time I had been desperate for a particular rider to win. Before this, I had always gone to support the Tour rather than an individual rider, or a team. Yes, I had my favourites, but none of them represented me. A victory for Pantani or any of the others would not change the whole perception of cycling in my country. A victory for Geraint Thomas would mean everything in Wales.

Even in previous stages, I'd never really thought Geraint would actually win the bloody thing and I had been reasonably relaxed. But now he could only lose if something terrible happened. When I saw one of the early riders veer straight off the course and into Espelette town centre, I had terrible visions of a similar calamity happening to Thomas, and it reminded me of an incident in the 1988 Tour de France. Robert Millar had looked set to win a Pyrenean mountain stage that year, with a finish in Guzet-Neige. The Scot was leading a three-man group in the final and looking very strong. However, Millar was confused by a *gendarme*'s directions and rode off course, missing out on a big win. What if that happened to Geraint Thomas?

Espelette is a nice enough village on the outskirts of Biarritz, but I couldn't see how it could cope with such a major event. As we approached, cars were backed up all along the main road for miles as spectators took their places along the course. But to be fair, the locals were well prepared and had earmarked a huge field nearby as a makeshift car park. Incredibly, they weren't even charging drivers to park there. That's one of the amazing things about the Tour – in general, it remains steadfastly uncommercial. The villagers could have made a killing, or raised money for a local charity, but they just wanted to provide a service.

We stood for a couple of hours on the roadside barriers watching some of the early rides, and met other Welsh people who had made the trip. Time Trial cyclists leave in reverse order of their GC ranking at two-minute intervals, and Geraint would be last to set off. A large grass bank provided a natural viewing point with a giant screen near the finish. This is where most people congregated, but we had other plans. We wanted to see history, and without a pass for the Grandstand, the best place we could be was beyond the finish line where we could celebrate with Geraint if the unimaginable happened. The course was hilly, but as long as it didn't rain, it should be OK. The last thing we wanted was a wet, slippery surface which could cause a crash. But the dark clouds overhead worried us and the road was already damp after an earlier downpour. Dumoulin, Froome and Roglič were predicted to take time on Thomas, but he was over two minutes ahead of all of them.

The presentation stage was erected on a roundabout on the outskirts of town. It was a pretty nondescript location to host an event where history would be made. The time trial run-in area was in front of the stage and we stood close by, joining the locals who had brought their stools and cool-boxes for a long day out. After cheering home some of the more familiar later riders, the nerves kicked in when Chris Froome started his ride. He was going very well, and so was Tom Dumoulin, who left soon after him. We watched the clock on the screen, without knowing what it really meant. We just knew they were going well, and were first and second place on the clock. Then we saw Geraint on the giant screen. "C'MON, GERAINT!" we shouted and waved our flags. Our French neighbours looked at us in shock. Some smiled, but others glowered. *"Allez Tom!"* they responded, lending their support to Dumoulin.

At the first checkpoint, Thomas was actually in front. I laughed and said it out loud for the first time: "He's going to win the Tour de France!" I said it again, louder, even confidently. "Geraint Thomas, from Wales, is going to win the Tour de France!" I started to celebrate inside. Then, as if to punish me for my hubris, he slipped on a corner and almost came down.

"WOOOAHH!" the crowd shouted, before breaking into laughter. I wasn't laughing. I blamed myself for tempting fate.

He was getting closer. At the next checkpoint he was still comfortable. He just had to stay on his bike. I saw his wife Sara being manoeuvred towards the line. "SARA! SARA!" I shouted. She spun around, grinning as she saw the flag. I raised my fist and shouted "He's going to win it!" She laughed and gave a little fist pump of her own.

Then in he came, across the line and straight into her arms. Geraint had no idea his wife would be there, and they were engulfed by photographers. We cheered and shouted and lifted the red dragon high above the crowds. We knew what we were seeing. We were witnessing the greatest moment in the history of sport in our little country. Geraint Thomas had won the Tour de France.

Thomas held his wife tightly and the tears flowed as he embraced Dave Brailsford at the finish line. His team manager, who grew up in Deiniolen in Snowdonia, gave him a Welsh flag to drape over his shoulders and offered an emotional interview in Welsh to S4C. Geraint was speechless, struggling to make sense of what had just happened.

> I can't believe it. I'm welling up, man. I don't know what to say. It's just overwhelming. I didn't think about it all race and now

suddenly I won the Tour, man. I felt good, I felt strong. I felt really good, actually. I heard I was up and I was maybe pushing a bit hard sometimes on the corners, so Nico [Portal, Team Sky's DS] told me to just relax, take it easy and just make sure I win the Tour, and so that's what I did.

It's just overwhelming. I can't speak, man. It's just incredible. I believed I could beat the guys here but to do it on the biggest stage of all over three weeks, it's insane. The last time I cried was when I got married. I don't know what's happened to me.

I hugged Scott for the first time since he had breathed on my back, and celebrated with my son and friends from home. There were fewer than 50 Welsh people there to share our joy, but plenty of Brits joined in the fun. Sadly, the French were less magnanimous, but nothing could spoil our day.

"Come on," said Scott. "Come to Paris!" He had a flight booked from Biarritz the next morning, but I would have to drive. But I had seen what I came to see, and I set off for the long drive back north to my family. I'd seen a Welshman win the Tour de France.

Houilles to
Paris Champs-Élysées

I HAD NEVER intended to go to Paris even if Geraint had won the race. I've been to the final stage just once, in 1994. To tell you you truth, after my experience on the Champs-Élysées that day, I wasn't that keen to go back.

I arrived very early to find that even several hours before the race, there were few places available on the railings at the side of the road. The finish line was inaccessible, of course, as even in those days the VIP grandstands excluded the hoi polloi. I've got no real complaints about that, as this is a free event to watch and it needs to be paid for somehow. I found myself a spot just beyond the finish line and settled down to lean on the barrier. It was only at this point that I noticed my neighbours had all brought collapsible stools and cool boxes full to the brim with refreshments. I had no seat and a single bottle of water. In my naivety I had assumed that I could restock with food and drink from nearby shops. I soon realised that if I left my space for a minute, it would be taken immediately by one of the hundreds of people that had slowly begun crowding the pavement. These days, I could keep myself occupied for hours with a mobile phone, but back then I was armed only with a polaroid camera and a copy of *L'Équipe*. The highlight of my morning was spotting Channel 4 presenter Phil Liggett on the course. I remember to this day what I shouted.

"MISTER LIGGETT! MISTER LIGGETT!"

He waved to the exceptionally polite man who was shouting to him from the crowd. If there is a running theme to my Tour de France experience, it is barking incoherently at somebody famous while they are just trying to get on with their lives. After a few hours I was desperate to answer a call of nature and asked my new friends to keep my place. I battled my way through the crowd, which was now 10-deep, and squirrelled my way back again 20 minutes later. Of course, my place had been taken and the people in the crowd were reluctant to let this ginger lad barge his way to the front. They blocked my way and elbowed me, and I gave as good as I got. Eventually I reached my spot, where I argued vociferously with a middle-aged *Madame* who was not giving up easily.

Honestly, it was all more trouble than it was worth, even though the rumble of the *peloton* as it passed repeatedly on the Champs-Élysées circuit was thrilling at first. And I did get a shot of one of my favourite riders: the Tashkent Terror, Djamolidine Abdoujaparov. So yes, I would go back again, but only if I had the luck of an acquaintance of mine who had rented a Paris apartment to find that its balcony overlooked the Champs-Élysées on race day. If I happened to be in Paris,

I'd watch the race on television in a bar, just popping out each time the *peloton* passed by outside.

But I had received an offer on the Col du Soulor which did turn my head. Scott had managed to wangle a VIP invitation from connections at Lotto-Soudal. But I had already driven all the way from Y Felinheli down to the Spanish border and it just felt like a step too far. I had left my wife and children on a campsite in the Loire Valley and there was no way I could spend any more time away from my precious family. Of course, I tested the water. But the patience of my generous, understanding wife had already been stretched too far. "We'd like you to come home now," she informed me quietly.

So I drove back to Brissac-Quincé while Scott flew on to Paris. His social media posts irritated me for days. He was somehow actually on the Champs-Élysées just metres in front of Geraint Thomas as he celebrated the greatest moment in Welsh sporting history. He'd even invited another friend of ours who had been a cycling fan for approximately 10 days. While they swanned around in the reflected glow of that yellow jersey, I watched the finish on TV back on that French campsite. The national broadcaster didn't even bother to show the ceremony. I'll admit it: I was jealous of Scott and Andy. I should have been there.

But, you know, I wasn't too upset. I had been there when it counted – to shout my support across the road in Pau, to cheer him up the final climb of the Tour, and to wave my flag when he crossed the line in Espelette. The 21st stage of the Tour is a procession for the winner, a victory parade, a pageant. Nonetheless, I would like to have seen it. I would like to have been there when Geraint stood on that podium with the Arc de Triomphe behind him. I would like to have seen him share his Welshness with the world.

Lance Armstrong understood the significance to our country better than many:

> I've never been to Wales... but to get up there – and you don't even see the yellow jersey, he's wrapped in the Welsh flag. It was neat to see. For them, this Welsh thing is a big deal.

Chris Froome seemed genuinely pleased about Geraint Thomas's success:

> It has been amazing to stand on the podium with Geraint Thomas up there. We have been teammates and friends for 10 years already. We've come so far together.

So how *did* a Welshman win the Tour?

I think if you look at Geraint Thomas's pathway as a rider, you can firstly see how he became *capable* of winning it. A lot of things had to happen for him to reach that podium.

Firstly, Debbie Wharton and Welsh Cycling had to start those cycling sessions at Maindy Centre. The young Geraint then needed the support of his family and volunteers to be able to travel, compete and win races. The decision to create a national lottery which then allocated funds to cycling allowed the formation of a national cycling academy where he could be nurtured. That academy broke down the cultural barriers which had stopped generations of talented young Welsh cyclists from trying their luck abroad. The decision to form Team Sky, with the biggest budget in world cycling, meant that he would train with and learn from the best. He would

149

ride with the best kit and improve by utilising the best sports science available.

But above all of course, he needed to be blessed with extraordinary ability and natural talent. He needed the discipline and drive to be able to dedicate himself to the sport. He knew that to win the Tour he would have to be able to climb. Anybody who's tried to lose weight knows how difficult that can be. Imagine trying to lose an extra 20 lbs when you're already a champion cyclist, exercising at the top level for hours every day. He must have lived on grass for six months. And this is a man who loves to eat Welshcakes, washed down with a few pints of lager. Imagine the self-discipline that took.

But we know that Geraint Thomas has always had that self-discipline. Crucially, at a very young age, he followed the orders of his coaches down to the letter, and it worked. He won races and gold medals because he listened. Now, at the age of 32, he was still willing to believe in sports science and coaching because it had worked for him throughout his career. If a dietician told him to eat 60 g of chicken and 43 grains of rice, then he was capable of doing that, if it meant he could win. I imagine the weighing scales are well used in the Thomas kitchen.

They say that a champion cyclist needs three attributes – good legs, a clear head and a strong heart. He had all three of those vital assets. Thomas was willing to suffer like a dog in order to improve. He recovered from the loss of a spleen, crashed and remounted numerous times, and rode the toughest event in the world with a broken pelvis. He refused to accept defeat and ignored pain. So Geraint Thomas went through all this, made all those sacrifices, and trained hard for 20 years to put himself in such incredible physical condition that he was able to win the Tour. But that didn't mean he *would* win the Tour. A lot of other things had to fall into place to create that scenario.

Firstly, he had to be arriving at the Tour in peak condition. And 2018 was the first year that he had been prepared by Team Sky as a potential winner. If Chris Froome's salbutamol issue had not been leaked, then Thomas would have been there as Plan B once again. But it was and Froome's appearance at the Tour was put in doubt. Team Sky prepared Geraint Thomas as their number one, just in case.

He then had to become team leader on the road. Thomas couldn't win it if Chris Froome started the race in good form. But Froome had ridden the Giro d'Italia and wasn't at his very best. As the race went on, it became apparent that Froome really wasn't as strong as Thomas. And after years of supporting others, the team were ready to pay him back with their own selfless sacrifice. Rowe, Castroviejo and Moscon controlled the early part of stages. Kwiatkowski, Poels and especially Bernal left it all in the mountains. By the end, even Froome was acting as an occasional *domestique* for the Welshman.

And what about his main rivals? They disappeared out of contention one by one. Landa, Yates, Nibali, Martin, Porte and Froome all crashed. Quintana was not in great form. That only left an inexperienced Roglič, and Tom Dumoulin. But Dumoulin was isolated in a weak team, and maybe still feeling the effects of riding the Giro d'Italia earlier in the year. Thomas rode through the 2018 Tour de France like Moses parting the Red Sea as all floundered around him. But he had to stay on his bike. And this was the most striking part of the Tour. While chaos reigned, while riders crashed on cobbles, on descents and sometimes just for no reason at all, Geraint stayed upright. The man who always crashed didn't crash.

And tactically, Geraint Thomas rode a perfect GC race. He was calm, wise and calculating. He didn't spend a second more on the front of the race than he had to. He took early bonus seconds when nobody else competed. He gambled that others would chase down moves, and they did. He identified Dumoulin as his only threat late on, and simply sat on his wheel until the end of each mountain stage, when he would pop out, sprint past and take more time. He demoralised the competition.

It's mind-boggling to think that all of these things had to fall into place for Geraint Thomas to win the Tour de France. But the truth is that every Tour winner has a similar tale. It takes an incredible combination of ability, training, the right circumstances and if not good luck, then an absence of bad luck, for anybody to win the world's greatest race. Fausto Coppi needed all of those things to win it, and so did Anquetil, Hinault and even Eddy Merckx. Anybody who has ever won the yellow jersey immediately becomes a titan, a legendary figure in worldwide sport. And this year, before my very eyes, the winner of the Tour de France was Geraint Thomas of Wales. Our greatest cyclist had won the greatest race.

Diolch, Geraint, *diolch*.

Acknowledgements

THANKS TO MY family for indulging my hobby, and not complaining when I abandoned our holiday to watch Geraint win the Tour. And thanks to Scott Thomas for persuading me to abandon my family to watch Geraint win the Tour.

Thanks to Dewi Owen of the excellent *Y Dihangiad* podcast for the proofreading, and Carolyn Hodges for the editing. This book was Lefi Gruffudd's idea, and I'm grateful for his support, along with that of the staff at Y Lolfa.

Finally, thanks to Geraint for making the unimaginable a reality.

Phil Stead
October 2018

Also by the author:

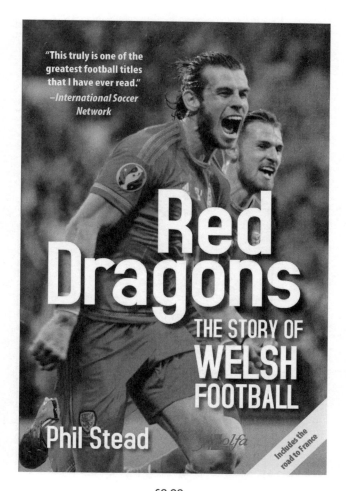

"This truly is one of the greatest football titles that I have ever read."
–International Soccer Network

Red Dragons

THE STORY OF WELSH FOOTBALL

Phil Stead

Includes the road to France

£9.99

Also from Y Lolfa:

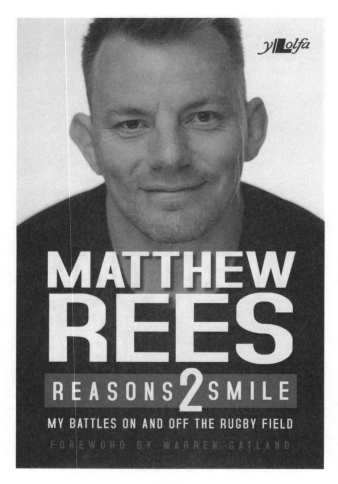

£9.99

GERAINT
Y CYMRO
A'R TOUR DE FRANCE

LLION IWAN

£6.99

Geraint Thomas is just one of a whole range of publications from Y Lolfa. For a full list of books currently in print, send now for your free copy of our new full-colour catalogue. Or simply surf into our website

www.ylolfa.com

for secure on-line ordering.

TALYBONT CEREDIGION CYMRU SY24 5HE
e-mail ylolfa@ylolfa.com
website www.ylolfa.com
phone (01970) 832 304
fax 832 782